CW00551265

RED
LIPSTICK

RED
LIPSTICK

The Men in My Life

LAXMI
with
POOJA PANDE

PENGUIN
VIKING

VIKING

USA | Canada | UK | Ireland | Australia
New Zealand | India | South Africa | China

Viking is part of the Penguin Random House group of companies
whose addresses can be found at global.penguinrandomhouse.com

Published by Penguin Random House India Pvt. Ltd
7th Floor, Infinity Tower C, DLF Cyber City,
Gurgaon 122 002, Haryana, India

First published in Viking by Penguin Random House India 2016

ISBN 9780670089185

Typeset in Minion Pro by Manipal Digital Systems, Manipal
Printed at Thomson Press India Ltd, New Delhi

www.penguinbooksindia.com

Vishnu is Mohini and Mohini, Vishnu.
This book is dedicated to our gods and goddesses . . .
Because they get it.

ॐ Contents ॐ

CONTENTS

❧ Glossary ❧

Perhaps some readers are unaware of the myriad terms and phrases that are a part of this book. To me, just as to so many others, they are the truths of my life, its facets, but to several others, they are plain jargon. So, here's a list of the common terms and abbreviations in *Red Lipstick*, so as to inform those who are ignorant and to dispel any confusion:

TG Transgender
MSM Men who have Sex with Men
LGBT Lesbian, Gay, Bisexual, Transgender
LGBTQ Lesbian, Gay, Bisexual, Transgender, Queer
DWS Dai Welfare Society
APNSW Asia Pacific Network of Sex Workers

❧ The Red Lipstick Monologue ❧

When I was born, the doctor checked my genitals and pronounced me a boy.

Who could foretell that a claim like that, a seemingly innocuous gesture, would mark me for life?

What we're assigned as at birth—male or female—is our gender. And somewhere along the way, we human beings decided that that gender would dictate our lives, steer us down certain paths, brand our behaviour, and inform almost all our choices—from something as trivial as the colour of your car to bigger decisions such as choosing a partner for life. Nobody ever seemed to realize that gender is nothing but an unromantic box.

And so it is that people like me, who fall nowhere in this binary, or somewhere in between, or even leap beyond—to me, the term 'transgender' has always implied 'transcending gender'—are considered misfits in society. We are termed 'abnormal', but as LGBT rights activist Ashok Row Kavi told me all those years ago when I, a boy myself, asked him why I liked men's crotches: 'The world around us is abnormal, baby. You are normal.'

As I was growing up, in the eyes of the world and those of my own family, I never gravitated towards 'manly' things. I loved to draw and paint, twirl around in lovely, flowy fabric, wear make-up and jewellery. My absolute passion, however, was dance. In dancing I was completely and utterly free. All of this meant, of course, that I was feminine. But the problem was that I was feminine *despite* being a boy. So when I wore bangles because they looked so good, red and shiny on my wrists, I would be told off by my friend's mother. Everyone's reactions around me seemed to indicate that I was acting like a girl, so I felt like a girl too. I would often refer to myself as one—'*Main abhi aati hoon*,' I would say, and immediately be reprimanded for doing that. '*Ladkiyon jaisi harkat mat kar* (Don't act like girls),' I would be told. When I decided to grow my hair because long hair is beautiful, it really disturbed my father. He made sure I had it cut, because '*Achche ghar ke ladke aise nahi karte* (Boys from good households do not behave this way).'

The world kept suggesting I was a girl, but my private parts indicated that I was a boy. And then there was the whole question of sexuality. I was attracted to boys—my first inklings and stirrings of lust came from noticing big, strong arms, the hint of a guy's moustache over his lips, billboards that advertised men's underwear—and I was puzzled. Was there a woman inside me who couldn't really express herself because of some last-minute mix-up that god did at the time of my birth?

Back then, in the early 1990s, the word 'gay' simply meant happy. Until one fine day, I was told that, in fact, that was who I was. Directed to Ashok for advice, I remember that day in Maheshwari Gardens so very well when seeing him and others like him and me around, I was overjoyed to have finally found an identity I could call mine wholeheartedly. I was not *chhakka*, *mamu*, *god*, or any of those terms hurled at me on a daily basis as abuses. I was gay. The world might still not like me for desiring someone of my own sex, but at least now there was certainty. For the first time in my life, I could set aside the crippling confusion and say to the world: 'I am a gay man.'

The certainty did not last long. Now the world expected me to behave in yet another way—once again I was confronted with parameters and boundaries. I could wear shirts and pants, but I had to look and act 'pansy'. And if I felt like wearing lipstick and a sari, it would mean I was 'doing drag'. I just liked the feel of the sari, and the way it draped over my body. Does there really have to be more to it, I wondered. As a gay man, I was also always supposed to be 'cruising' other gay men—to be on the lookout for sex almost constantly. How exhausting! Is that any way to live? And why is it all only about sex?

I wondered about all this as I went on with my life, checking the boxes I was tagged under as a gay man, as a drag queen. But the question of my identity, that dialogue with myself, remained unanswered, unaddressed. Who am I when it's just me, alone in my room? Who am I for the world? Are these two selves different, do they have to be?

I am thirty-seven today and, over the years, I don't know if I have reached a place closer to the answer; I don't know if I ever will. But if there is one identity I stay true to, it is the one that was created almost seamlessly— it is the Laxmi the world demanded when I went out to make my voice heard, to talk about the rights of transgenders. The persona of Laxmi the activist that was formed as much by the world I was interacting with, as by my own efforts. The supremely confident Laxmi who wears gorgeous saris, expensive make-up and perfume, who projects an image of absolute self-assurance, travels the length and breadth of the country and attends international conferences, gives speeches at queer pride parades, delivers TED Talks, is interviewed by the likes of *Guernica* and Salman Rushdie. So many doors that were closed to me, that were firmly shut, opened to this Laxmi. The creation of this persona has played an incredibly important role in my story, in the journey of my life—I began to enjoy being this Laxmi. And this Laxmi got things done. So she is as much for the world as for me.

If there is one role for me, the one big cause I know I am meant for, the raison d'être of my existence, it is that of an activist. I firmly believe that even if you have the best laws, unless you change the mindset of people, nothing will change. And that is what true activism means to me. That's why I can never be a 9–5 activist, I don't understand that, I am and can only be a 24/7 activist. Which is why, whatever the circumstances in my personal life, in public I have to be that—*the* Laxmi. Once I step out of my personal space, I cannot be merely myself. I have to be in the garb of that strong activist Laxmi because, inadvertently, I have come to represent a community of millions of people in this country. People look up to me and I have to fulfil the responsibilities of the role that has been given to me. No matter what I'm dealing with in my personal life, in public, I always go as Laxmi, the strong unbreakable activist nobody can mess with. In fact if I am going through a difficult time personally, I act even stronger when I don the persona. When I'm completely alone, all by myself, I'm not sure what feeling I am most comfortable with, who I feel is completely and only me. I ask myself many questions: Who am I? What am I? Then later I think, 'Fuck it. I am Laxmi.' That's my persona; there is no room for doubt.

When Rama was leaving Ayodhya to begin his fourteen-year exile in the forest, such was his popularity, so great the devotion of his people towards him, that the entire kingdom followed him to the outskirts of the city. Touched by their support, Rama turned around and told his subjects, 'I request all the men and women gathered here who truly love me, to please return to their homes. Once the duration of my exile is complete, I shall be back with you.' At the completion of his exile, when Rama returned, he saw that there were several people still waiting at the same spot on the outskirts of Ayodhya where he had bid them farewell all those years ago. These were the hijras, my brethren, those who did not return to their homes, since Rama had implored only the men and women to do so and they were neither. Overwhelmed by their dedication, Rama granted them, and future generations of hijras, a boon—we would have the power to grant both blessings and curses to men and women, which would always come true. When hijras were patronized and indulged by royalty, they were not only visible but respected. It is this history and tradition of the hijra culture—rich, strong, textured—in our country that I found myself most drawn to. A tradition in which even the mighty, macho warrior Arjuna could don the garb and identity of a woman and become Brihannala effortlessly. A culture that offers us characters such as Shikhandi, the transgender who managed to thwart the invincible Bhishma. Where the ultimate male god, whose linga unmarried girls worship, praying and observing fasts for strong, able-bodied men as their husbands, also acknowledges his feminine self, and even embraces it, literally. They subsume within one another, fuse to become Shiva–Shakti—the Ardhanareshwara. A history that speaks of hijras in eminent positions, as political advisors to kings, administrators, generals, and guardians of harems.

I embraced the identity of hijra deliberately; it was a conscious choice I made, one that not too many understood. Why, after all, would a male child belonging to an affluent, upright Brahmin family initiate himself into a cult, a tradition, a section of society that's much reviled by the mainstream? Why, indeed? It is seldom by choice that most hijras are hijras—it is, in fact, the lack of education and opportunities that forces many to find refuge in the hijra world. A lack that I, by the grace of god and my parents, never faced. So why would I, a privileged boy, become a hijra?

I was barely twenty when I met Lawrence Francis, aka Shabina, back in 1998. She was the first hijra I met and became close to. I used to work as a model coordinator in those days, and Shabina was the brother of a friend who worked as a model. Until then I was like any other person, frightened and somewhat repulsed by hijras. I met Shabina at the Chhatrapati Shivaji Terminus station and coaxed her into going with me to Café Mondegar for a bite and a chat. I asked her many questions and learnt a lot about hijras in the process—the history, rituals, lifestyles, sources of income, the concept of *gharana*s, how your guru is like your parent, you are the chela, and it becomes a family. A few days later, I went to Byculla where the head of Shabina's Lashkar gharana, Lata *naik*, held court. Nervous and unsure, I finally gathered the courage to ask those assembled there, 'I want to become a chela. How much is the fee?' To my surprise, they all burst out laughing. Lata guru, who went on to become my guru, said, 'There is no fee, child. If you want to become my chela, come.' My initiation ceremony, the *reet*, followed soon after—I was given two green saris, which are known as *jogjanam* saris signifying the inculcation into a new way of life, and crowned with the community dupatta.

Whenever I hear the term 'transgender', which we hear so often these days, I always feel that it implies 'transcending gender'. Identifying as transgender, I connect with being hijra the most—the word 'hij' refers to a holy soul and the body in which it resides is 'hijra', hence they say the soul is hijra. As hijra, I can access both states of being—and I can also go beyond. In my strongest moments, I feel what a man feels, the power games that they like to play. And when I'm shining in my femininity, driving men crazy, I feel more like a woman than even the most womanly of women one could imagine. Like Cleopatra, or Umrao Jaan—both ultimate symbols of femininity.

I would really question things at one point. What is it about me that attracts men, I would wonder. These 'straight', patriarchal men. I am not a woman; I am feminine, but I am not a woman biologically, so what are these men about? So many men who've called me mother or sister have turned to me on an evening when they were drunk or when they thought I was drunk and have wanted to sleep with me. But I don't need motherfuckers or sisterfuckers in my life. 'Get the hell out of here!' I would respond. They were ready to sacrifice everything to be in bed with me, even our relationship. I wondered then how that would happen— all these men were, in the eyes of the world and their own, heterosexual. And then I realized that the notion of heterosexual is, in itself, questionable. If you think about it, a woman is complete—she is XX and therefore complete. It is the man who is XY and hence has the woman in him. This 'manliness', then, is just a show, nothing but a convenient construct, a pretence to keep patriarchy alive, to keep women tamed. I am fortunate to be able to traverse through both genders so well. It is why I understand patriarchy inside out, and why I can empathize with the things women do, and how they think, act and behave.

Being a woman is so beautiful though—if I could always stay in that state of being, if I had the choice, I probably would. Again, I am not alone in this. Our heritage is full of stories that tell us how being a woman is a preferred state of being and existence. Take, for instance the story of King Bhangashvana, recounted in the Mahabharata, who lived his life both as a man and as a woman and who, when faced with the ultimate choice, opted to be a woman. And this was a king! There is also that unmistakable element of mystery about a woman, which is so alluring, which everyone wants and desires, and something that men can never experience. *Tera charitra swayam Brahma nahi samajh paaye*, they say—the Creator himself could not fathom womanhood and a woman's character.

Being a woman is not easy in our culture, however. I often wonder how I come across as a woman. Slutty and available? Perhaps. But why? Is it because ever since I had the choice about my body and who I would give it to, I have only slept for pleasure? Or because I have opinions, strong ones, that I'm not scared to voice?

Women always have an image that men or the world constructs for them—it's how they see them and how women see themselves. But that's not how I feel. I think everyone creates their own parameters and boundaries and they live and function within them—*charitra ke maap dand*. And it's the same for me. As far as I'm concerned, I am the Ganga, the holy Ganga. My purity cannot be measured by society's standards. My purity is to my own self, to my own parameters. It is how I have conducted myself throughout my life and continue to. I decide my own standards and I abide by them. I have my own sense of integrity that's very strong and in place, which nobody else has decided for me. My spirituality is to my soul, and it is for me. It should work for me. The world cannot have a say in that.

THE CREATOR

The Maker, the Source, the Generator

·◇· **Surya** ·◇·

Brahma is the great Creator/Life, a mystic drama

Even before I was born, there was a rift in my family. Perhaps in anticipation of what was to follow.

My mother, Vidyawati Tripathi, who came from a wealthy family, spent the first year of her married life in just two saris—having married my father only because of the Tripathi family's name and their social standing in the Brahmanical world of Gorakhpur. Once when she was pulling the *pallu* of her sari to don the *ghunghat* over her head—a practice followed by the women of our household—the hem of the sari tore. My father's eldest brother was enraged at this—'How can you do this? We can't afford to buy new clothes all the time. Do you know how much your husband earns?' His wife, my aunt, had an overpowering personality as well. She was not a family woman at all, questioning everyone's actions, and trying to destroy the household. So there were quarrels and arguments all the time at home. My mother, of course, always maintained: 'Whatever my husband says is right.' You know how they say that the mother is the mother earth, and the father, the sky. My father was that complete sky to my mother. And to me as well.

Chandradev Chandinath Tripathi, my father, was, I believe, the perfect man, because he created all three genders: my elder sister, Rukmini, a woman; my younger brother Shashi, a man; and me. He was the archetypal man, a *mard*—strong, handsome, tall. He was very patriarchal, very strict, and he loved his family, his entire family. Everything he did was for the family. But when he was suffering from cancer, nobody from the village even came to see him, let alone ask us if we needed any help. I sometimes feel that the last year of his life must have been the saddest—especially those last few months. He sacrificed all his life for his whole family and what did he get in return? I can feel his pain. If only he had thought about his own wife and children back then, and throughout his life, we would have been better off financially today—there would have been good money. But for him, it was always 'family first'.

When my grandfather put the ancestral land up for mortgage, my father came to Bombay to support himself and the family. He was only sixteen when he started at the JK File Company as a worker. After his elder brother's death, he took on the mantle of the head of the family—taking complete responsibility for everyone, always taking care of everyone. He brought his brothers to Bombay when he could afford it—one went on to work at Mahindra. He did so much for my older cousin, Shyam Mohan Tripathi, after his father passed away.

I was a very sickly child, falling ill often and suffering serious bouts of asthma; I'm still prone to them. It was my father who took the utmost pains in bringing me up and making sure I was fine. He did anything and everything he could, leaving no stone unturned in trying to find a solution to my medical problems, in making sure I got the treatment I needed. I still remember the time he had taken permission from my school to take me for acupuncture treatment for my asthma. The doctor was only available during school hours and Papa would come on his Bajaj scooter to my school and take me to the doctor. Those were rainy days and he would first make me wear my raincoat and cover me up properly before taking me to the clinic in Bhandup. His only concern was that his 'bachcha' should be fine, that nothing should happen to me. I have seen my father having sleepless nights and going to work in the morning, with only one worry: Was I, his child, still alive? For so many years, it was his only concern—that I become better, that I don't suffer. And this was the time when my father used to do overtime at work, which means 18-hour workdays! He went from being a worker to a foreman, and eventually he became the union leader. Such a hard-working man.

But the absolute beauty of my father, what was simply amazing about him, was that he never questioned me. There he was, a part of such an orthodox Brahmin family, patriarchal to the core, and there I was, his firstborn male child, his eldest son, oozing femininity. The world would taunt him so much about my sexuality, but he would simply ignore it. People would say to him, '*Tripathi ji bada yeh woh bante hain, khandaan ka naam vagehra, woh toh apne ladke ko sambhaal bhi nahi paaye. Hijron mein chala gaya bachcha* (Mr Tripathi talks so much about the family name and this and that, but he couldn't keep his own son under control. He went and joined the hijras).' He was plagued with this kind of talk for years together. It must have been absolutely torturous, but he was never affected by it, and even if he was, he never ever expressed it in my presence. Fathers rail at their children all the time, don't they? Or make their children feel like they owe it to them, but never my father—he never did that. Fathers have the power to ruin your life; they can force you to do things, exploit their 'because-I-said-so' authoritarian status, but never my father. He was once asked in an interview, 'Don't you feel ashamed that you're a Brahmin and your eldest son is a hijra?' And he replied, 'Why should I feel ashamed? No educated man or woman goes into their son's or daughter's bedrooms to see what they are doing there, do they? Laxmi Narayan has his own choice to do what he pleases. My child is not handicapped, my child is not mentally challenged, my child is different, his sexuality is different and that doesn't bother me. Nobody throws away a desi ghee laddoo, whether it comes out perfectly round or misshapen. My child is and will always be my child.'

When I joined the hijra community and he came to know about it, he confronted me and said I should get married. 'How can I do that?' I replied. 'Spoil not only my own life, but also that of the woman who would marry me!' I told him I would rather kill myself, and he had tears in his eyes. He finally only said, 'All right. Do whatever you want to do, I won't pressurize you, but please do it from home.' How many parents have the balls to tell their children that? Those who belong to the upper crust of society, even they won't be able to say this to their children, they are such hypocrites. People who keep talking about being progressive are actually not quite as progressive as they would have us believe. When he heard that I would change into a sari after leaving the house in the mornings, he told me I should wear it at home itself. 'If someone on the street asks me today, "Do you know Laxmi is wearing a sari?" I should be able to say, "Yes, I know. And it's red."' There was a time when dance was my life, but my father always supported me, he never objected to anything. He never came to see any of my dance shows—that would be asking too much, even from him—but he gave me the liberty to do whatever I wanted.

When I appeared on the TV show *Sach Ka Saamna*, one of the questions they asked me was if I had been sexually abused. My father looked absolutely gutted when I answered yes. I had never told my parents, of course, and he was shattered, in a way, to learn that his child had suffered like that. When that episode was aired, my father was suffering from cancer, and he was recovering after his first operation. It was heart-wrenching for me to watch him, and many people still remember my father from that episode—that he had the guts to sit through that. When the shoot of *Sach Ka Saamna* was over, he never asked me who it was that had molested me. He simply looked at me, I looked at him, and he knew I was okay, and that was it. He realized that his child was now strong enough, that I had overcome it. The best thing about our relationship was the silence that played between us often. No words were spoken, only looks. A lot of silence. You know how it is with fathers, they're slightly distant, and you're talking to the mother all the time. But we, Papa and I, would communicate without speaking.

Eventually, we became like friends. I would tell him who I was dating, he would meet my boyfriends. My friends, hijras, they would all sit and talk with him for hours. If someone came to meet me and I wasn't around, he would always ask them to make themselves comfortable even if he didn't approve of them, sit them down, chat with them. In fact, when we had problems, my friends would complain to my father about me, because they knew he was the only one who could exert some control over me. I was scared of him also, of course—it was the respect *wala* fear we all feel for our fathers.

For me, he was the complete man who brought me into this world. If it weren't for him, I would have been standing in a brothel, selling my body. I would have been HIV positive by now. I lost him to cancer and I don't think I'll ever reach a place in my life where I won't miss him. I haven't yet understood it fully—that he is no more. When I go back home in the evenings, my mother comes into my room, because she knows that I don't like entering hers—it was there that I lost my father and stepping inside it always reminds me of him. When I am alone during the day, or feeling lonely, or when I'm doing something as banal as brushing my teeth, I find myself getting lost looking in the mirror, and questioning: Why did he have to go so early? Is he really gone? I know it was his destiny, and my fate, and he went. But it's hard to come to terms with it completely.

That man always loved me. Can you imagine how strong one has to be to give that kind of love, to love someone like that? It can only be a father. It was my father.

In the form of the sun, it is Surya

Atharv Nair is *the* person behind Laxmi. I believe we first met at a cruising spot in Thane that was frequented by gay men. We were introduced by Sangeeta, a hijra, who died later. Atharv was the first dark-complexioned guy I had an affinity towards. He was always so chivalrous—he would walk me to the rickshaw stand. Atharv was studying at the Tata Institute of Social Sciences at the time and was doing a project on transgenders. Back then—this must have been 1999–2000—the term 'transgender' didn't even exist, there were limited queer studies and close to zero resources available. The Internet had just come to India. The only terms people knew were effeminate *koti* or gay. Atharv identifies himself as trans and has never really felt like a man. Given the apparent lack of resources then, he decided to take it up as a project so he could study it properly and comprehend the problem. Back then, there were no legitimate spaces to meet people of the community, or even like-minded people, and Thane became an informal hub to meet people. Atharv lives an hour outside of Thane and he would come to meet people. The Thane bus stand was a famous hang-out spot for this!

We met again properly through Vijay Pawar who was heading the Humsafar Outreach programme, an organization working with the MSM community. I had just begun my second consecutive term as president of the DWS and I needed someone to help me with my work because I wasn't good at all the computer-related stuff. That's when Atharv came and joined me and started doing documentation. I was absolutely floored by his intelligence, and to date, he is definitely one of the smartest, sharpest intellectuals I know.

Because he is well educated and can speak fluent English, Atharv can successfully hobnob with the elite, and because he is grounded and totally at ease with the lower-middle class as well, he can work comfortably with anyone in the community. He always says that he has no hang-ups and can also become like the furniture in the room and just observe and study and read. These became his strengths even in his work.

It was as if Atharv came for a project, but really was a blessing in my life, and so he never left. He became completely entrenched in the DWS. Unlike many in his position, he wasn't simply looking to finish a project, submit it, get the marks and move on. He started to look at his work in the DWS as a way of actually doing some good and making a real difference for the community. Atharv has a deep passion for the cause. He has always believed that transgenders have a lot of talent that never comes to the fore due to a lack of opportunities. For instance, compared to transgenders, gay men don't find themselves getting short-changed as much at the workplace because they can conveniently switch over when required—they can be all-male in the work environment if needed and carry on, being given the same opportunities as, say, straight men. But trans people are visibly trans, it's who they are, so they can't suddenly transform themselves and behave according to prescribed norms around the time of promotions and appraisals at work. Even though Atharv and I are different as people—he's quite sorted and I'm all over the place—we worked well with each other. This was mostly because our cause was the same and there was a genuine meeting of the minds: we both believe that trans people need to have opportunities, and these have to be created through work.

We worked together on Avahan, the Bill & Melinda Gates Foundation-sponsored programme, which targeted interventions—blood testing and distribution of condoms—specifically within the transgender community. These were generally hijras who were in three lines of work—*badhaai* (when hijras go to homes to bless newlywed couples or a newborn baby), *mangti* (when they beg and threaten with curses), and *dhandha* (sex work). It was a big project and we did well, but we felt stuck after a while. There is rigidity in the hijra community and the DWS followed that to the letter. But you need change to evolve. And of course you need the structure to function. Atharv was the one to understand and realize this and envision a future. I was having a tough time with Lata guru in those days, my guru in the hijra community, who had started the DWS. I was trying to be myself while simultaneously attempting to live by the rules and regulations of the community, being monitored every second of my life by Lata guru. It was slowly becoming impossible for me. Lata guru did not trust me completely and would question my actions and decisions constantly. At the same time, Atharv had begun to feel very strongly that our work had to change its mission and narrative.

We discussed this at length and concluded that we both wanted to work on a broader scope and with complete flexibility and innovation, and keep up with the times as well. Targeted interventions depend heavily on funding and make you answerable to the funders— the moment you take their money, you're bound to them. But that didn't seem like something we wanted to do; we wanted to actually make a difference. We firmly believed that transgenders had to be accepted into society—Atharv would say it to me often, 'Laxmi, we do exist. So let's create something together, where we can work on this properly, as a registered organization.' When I decided to leave the DWS and Lata guru, she said it was only because of Atharv that I had taken that decision. She remarked on how loyal I had been to her, and claimed that he poisoned my mind against her and the DWS. But the truth is that Atharv came into my life at a time when I was lonely and feeling absolutely claustrophobic in the hijra culture. It was he who made me see that, and realize that I was not being true to myself.

'You are not *this*, Laxmi. Why does that free-spirited Laxmi have to live like this, in this situation?' he would question me. And he was right.

That's how Astitva came into being. It is our *astitva*— our identity, our self, our being. We left the DWS and in 2006 we established Astitva, a non-profit organization working with sexual minorities—Atharv, Kiran More, my hijra friend who was the DWS treasurer, and I—with very little money in our pockets, but a lot of goodwill, noble intentions and the passion to do good, solid work. Atharv said that he did not want any position, but I put my foot down and said he should be the general secretary. Astitva means existence, identity, and this organization was all about our fight for our existence, and the key people needed to be playing key roles, I was certain of that.

We started off determined to work with all sexual minorities. Most organizations were specific—gay, MSM, TG—but we wanted to include everybody. So we could see it as one cause and act accordingly. We even had bar girls in our organization. The politics around queer activism sickened us and we wanted to build a new space for it. Gradually, with me being hijra and hijras being the most visible TG community in India, it made greater sense for us to work more exclusively with them, but always work towards the bigger picture. This marked a new chapter in my activism—from being on the streets to working in the more organized style of an activist. It was like sorting myself out.

It was very difficult in the beginning—to even just break on to the scene and be acknowledged. We were never invited to important meetings, nor were we kept in the loop. We had to barge in on sessions and meetings so many times, make our contacts, start our own networks. It has taken us very long and a lot of work to get here.

In the beginning, we didn't have much work and almost no capital. Atharv would take on other assignments for money—conduct small consultancy sessions with colleges and universities, coordinate and run group discussions and meetings, make presentations. I would do dance performances and make money. Atharv was always the one thinking a few steps ahead, and he was very sure that I had to be the face and persona of Astitva, so he would keep pushing me to be visible in places and gatherings. He would tell me, 'You should do this, you should take that invite, you should go meet so and so.' Contrary to popular opinion and unlike what people think, I actually don't jump on to any and every opportunity I get. I am always hesitant at first, my initial response is wariness. I need to be certain of it, and Atharv knows that I need to be pushed. He did a lot of that in our initial days of making contacts and network-building, because there is really no other way. The growth of Laxmi the activist is absolutely linked with placing Laxmi in the right places, and that's mostly been Atharv's work. Of course, just placing me or sending me somewhere wouldn't have been enough; it was I who had to take it forward after all. I too have worked very hard to be where I am today, but it simply would not have been possible if Atharv hadn't been in my life and hadn't arrived when he did.

Our early days were challenging. There were so many times when we didn't even step out of the office for days and days. So many times when we didn't have money for the auto fare to go and attend meetings. There was so much we had to learn, so much we didn't know but we were always keen and enthusiastic about it all. We were never afraid of our ignorance, or ashamed of it. And we achieved a lot, right from organizing the first transgender pageant to getting a rights-based organization.

I remember when T.R. Meena, from the Ministry of Social Justice and Empowerment, wanted to meet me. Atharv studied to understand what it was about and then told me that I should go ahead with the meeting. I spoke to Ernest (Noronha, UNDP India) and a couple of other lawyer friends before attending the meeting. It proved to be an extremely fruitful interaction for us, for Astitva, for the cause. In getting a steering committee for TGs.

We founded Astitva as a fight for our existence, and I think we did achieve a lot. We are the youngest civil rights movement that got a Supreme Court verdict, which had a bill passed by the Rajya Sabha. We are, every day, achieving what we set out to. The Maharashtra government's policy on women is the first in the entire world to have a chapter on TGs and sex workers. Nobody else had been able to do that before us. The NALSA judgement in our favour has, as part of its mandate, camps for judicial and legal services and consultancy and we were the first ones to implement that in Thane. *(Details of this on page 197.)* We got an award for it from NALSA, where we were presented as a success story. So we've done a lot of pioneer work, and initiated programmes. I was the intervenor in the Supreme Court NALSA case. After founding Astitva, I went to the United Nations representing the sex workers of the Asia-Pacific region—that was a big milestone in my life. And after that, I was everywhere—representing India and talking about our rights.

We're still struggling of course—railway tickets still only have M and F choices. Basic amenities like toilets are again only M and F. But we are working towards change and working hard. Things have altered, they are evolving, and there is hope.

Atharv has been the optimist I've always needed—telling me not to worry about things ahead of time, not to fret about crossing the bridge until we come to it! For my first international conference, it was Atharv who forced me to go to the passport office in Thane—I was so wary and anxious about what they would say to me, and if they would reject my application. But he was the one who persuaded me to go for it and even accompanied me on the day. In that sense I feel we also balance each other in some ways in our work—he is more practical, rational and he doesn't get worked up easily. I can get very emotional about things. And you need both to make it work. I think we're better halves that come together as a whole; there's turmoil too, but when we work together, we make things happen, and I get the feeling that there isn't anything that we can't achieve. And I know that he feels the same way.

We have our differences too, on so many points. We have a mutual understanding on topics that we know we should avoid speaking to each other about, because no matter what I say, he'll have a counter-argument for it! Like with my current love interest Viki (Thomas)—I know how Atharv feels about him and it's not favourable.

Atharv also has a degree in psychology and thinks that he can analyse people by their actions and behaviour quite accurately. And in all his interactions with Viki, he has found him fake and pretentious and untrustworthy. Also, ever since I had a bad episode with Viki that turned violent, he has completely given up on the guy. He hasn't spoken to Viki since and he never will—he has made that clear to me and Viki too. That way Atharv is quite straightforward. He told me, 'If you are happy and you know what you're doing, it's fine. No one has the right to interfere with your happiness and of course you should have a happy and fulfilling personal life . . . But just remember that you are the one who has to handle it yourself. If something goes wrong, you'll have to come out of it. I'll be there to help, but ultimately, it'll have to be you. Basically, deal with it yourself, it'll be your headache.' He also feels that I should be with someone who'll move me up in public life, help with my larger cause because that's the stage I'm at currently. Maybe because he has worked so hard in bringing me where I am today.

Atharv is my soul. I'm so blessed to have an angel like him beside me practically all the time. I bitch about him all the time too and I'm constantly angry with him. He doesn't answer my calls and he's a pain in the ass, but we have an amazing relationship. I respect his loyalty a lot, I never question anything he does—his loyalty towards me and my trust in him can never ever be doubted, no matter what. He is the biggest moral support I have. We communicate on a special plane—he knows what I'm about to say even before I have actually said it. He knows me so well that he can read me like a book. If someone asks me a question when he's around, he knows exactly how I'll respond. And it's the same for him because I know him so well. We've been together for fifteen years; it's such a beautiful relationship and it's completely platonic. We have never been separated. I know people feel uncomfortable with our relationship and have assumed lots of times that we are together as couple. The fact that we often stay in the same room when we travel for work might contribute to that, but all that doesn't matter to us.

He's been there in all my moments—when I was feeling low in life, he was there by my side; when I was happy and celebration was in the air, then too he was with me. Because he is like family now, he also understands mine, especially my parents. When my father was alive, he got along well with Atharv. And my mother of course keeps complaining to him about me. Atharv understands that the parents of transgenders experience the same trauma as the child. It's a similar 'Why me?' persecution and paranoia. So he has become the person my family vents to when I'm not available, which is often because of my work. He'll hear them out, give them his opinion, even pacify them if needed. And when he gets some time alone with me, he'll mention it to me. Amidst all our work-related talk, he'll also tell me that such and such thing is troubling Mummy, so maybe I should not do it or how I should be careful. He's sensitive to everyone's feelings too—when he speaks to Mummy, he'll immediately switch to calling me Raju (my childhood nickname), even though he always calls me Laxmi.

Atharv has the power to influence me greatly and he knows it but it's not in his nature to manipulate anybody, least of all me. With me, if he does it, he'll only use it for work—something that he feels would benefit us, our work, the community and our cause. That's it. He's all about work that way—he's at it all the time, 24/7. His personal life is non-existent. If he's at home, it means he's sleeping.

Over the years, he has mastered the art of working with me. If he needs to make a point with me, or wants me to notice something, or take action about something, or if something needs my immediate attention, he won't tell me ten times, because he knows that I won't even bother then. Instead, he'll pick just the right moment to present it to me, very subtly, very softly, but very firmly. Like 'Laxmi, do this now and only then can I move forward on this.' Or he'll say, 'If you're not figuring this out now, then don't tell me later that something wasn't done.' Or if he thinks that I'm being unnecessarily dramatic about something, then he'll tell me that too. He'll point it out as a weakness—that I'm getting carried away, or being too emotional, and since I'm prone to hasty decisions how I should wait and think it over. He also knows I'm a queen—and he'll put me in my place by just ignoring me! In his mind I know he's thinking, 'Now she'll come around and get back in action!' So Atharv has his killer strategies!

I am totally dependent on Atharv—he does all the work, everything. I am just the business card, the face, the persona.

Heaven, and Earth, and Living Nature/Are but
Masks of Brahma

Manhood is generally associated with strength, but to me it's all a state of mind, regardless of your gender and whether you were born what the world considers a 'man' or a 'woman'. Everything is *prakriti* (nature), and to me all nature or creation is feminine—hence men, too, are feminine, because they are within prakriti; they are subsumed by creation, nothing is beyond prakriti. There is no such thing as *all* man, or *only* man, in my mind. Biologically born men who were assigned the 'male' gender at birth, and who live and grow up as men in the world, do so only to become the custodians of patriarchy, a system that came into being only to suppress women. I don't see how that makes them strong. And on the other hand, those who are pronounced 'female' at birth and grow up as women are considered naturally nurturing or caring, which is somehow translated into weakness. But to me that doesn't mean they are weak—women who are tender and nurturing can be very, very strong.

There have been several women in my life who were 'like men' in that sense—with strong identities and powerful personalities—yet at the same time, were extremely nurturing.

Chhaya Patil is one such woman. As someone who really built the foundation of Laxmi, she will always be the ultimate creator for me.

Chhaya belongs to a Maratha caste. Her upbringing was quite orthodox and her background is fairly conservative. A very traditional lady, a housewife who, through the sheer strength of her character and mind, succeeded in pulling me out of a certain way of thinking about myself. Chhaya and I met in 1993—at a time when I had little faith in myself, and no confidence, and it was she who convinced me to start my own dance classes. She had more confidence in my abilities as a dancer than I did. And that conviction really gave birth to the assured and professional dancer that I then went on to become.

I used to teach at the dance classes conducted by Baby Johnny, where Chhaya's child used to come for lessons. When I went to the sets of *Boogie Woogie* once, to participate as a member of the audience, she met me there and told me, 'You are fairly good yourself. Why do you need to be in somebody else's class, or just an audience member at this show? You must start your own dance class. Why aren't you doing that?' She would leave her other child at home—a mere baby then, just two years old—to come and meet me, and try to convince me about this. She refused to let it go, and eventually I did start my own classes. They went on to become successful, and that gave Chhaya a lot of joy—she's someone who's always happy in my happiness.

At times, she would get furious with me for being too hijrotic, as I call it—a blend of hijra and erotic, of course!—or acting too hijrotic. She would even tell me to seek help from a psychologist because she thought I might have some specific issues that made me behave so femininely, despite being a man. I remember when I started growing my hair, my father requested her to ask me to cut it, because he did not want to confront me directly. And she just came and told me, in her straightforward manner, '*Laxmi, baal kaato. Papa ko achcha nahi lag raha hai* (Laxmi, get your hair cut. Papa doesn't like it).' And for her, I did cut my hair. It was the first time in my life I did that for anyone.

We became very close over the years. I would call her 'didi'; I still do. She is the only person in my life, besides my own sister Rukmini, who ties me a rakhi each year. Earlier, she would gift me a kurta each year, but around six or seven years ago, that changed and for the first time ever, she brought me a sari for Rakhi. Ever since then, she's been giving me a sari each year and adding to my collection.

That is the ultimate love, isn't it? To accept me for what I am, who I am—to me that is a very big thing and a true mark of love. It'd be very easy to say that I became a hijra one fine day and that everyone accepted me unquestioningly—but that's not the reality. I know that for Chhaya didi, buying me a sari is a very, very big deal. And were it not for her faith and confidence in me, I would never have had the gumption or sense to embrace the dancer in me.

Brahma satyan/Jagat mithya

I met Andrew Hunter, president and founding member of the Scotland-based Global Network of Sex Work Projects (NSWP), on my visit to Bangkok as part of the civil society task force of the APNSW, which fights the exploitation of sex workers in Malaysia, Thailand, Singapore, India, Pakistan, Bangladesh and Nepal. Andrew worked extensively with Thailand's *kathoys* (lady boys) and had also started the NGO Scarlet Alliance to press for their rights. He was an immense inspiration, and it wouldn't be enough to merely say that he was a major influence on me. He was my teacher, and the person who made me fully realize the activist inside me. He had complete faith in me. It was Andrew who taught me about activism, about the politics, the work, how to really *be* an activist. He trusted in the calibre of Laxmi and really gave me the confidence to believe in myself, to believe that I could do it. Because *he* thought I could do it, *I* thought I could do it. And gradually, I *knew* I could do it—that confidence became a fire in my belly that stoked my ambition and kept me going. He would always say to me, 'You are not supposed to be scared of anybody. We are activists. We may die, but our voices will always remain strong.'

Andrew promoted me everywhere possible. He taught me the ropes, the ways to move around in the social development sector, how to ensure that your voice is heard. He was my true godfather. He polished Laxmi, and turned the rough stone into a glittering diamond. I could call him at any time, even in the middle of the night, to seek clarification on some details or the specifics of something, or for advice, and he would always be available. Like a true teacher, guide and philosopher.

He often said to me, 'Laxmi, I want to see you in Parliament one day.' I always followed his instincts and tried my best to live up to his expectations.

Sadly, Andrew passed away in 2013. I still remember his funeral, and his partner Dale—he was so loved by everyone because of his stupendous work. I miss him so much as a mentor, but in a way he will always be with me till my last breath, because he brought to life the spark in me. I really wish he was alive today so he could see me in the Country Coordinating Mechanisms (CCM) of the Global Fund. He would have been so happy.

Andrew was the person who made Laxmi famous, who made Laxmi *Laxmi*. Laxmi the activist was born only because of him.

THE PRESERVER

The Protector, the Operator,
the Custodian of Life and Living

·◈· **Agni** ·◈·

*And he who understands it aright will rather preserve its
life than destroy it*

In Indian culture, especially in the Hindu tradition, hijras are considered *upadevatas* or sub-gods—they rank higher than mortals, men and women, saints and sadhus as well. I have read and studied a number of religious books in which we, the third gender, are not only present and visible but a legitimate and significant part of the social order. So nobody, I believe, can wipe us out and deny our existence. Society wants to marginalize us—a law of the land that came into being during British rule over India, not before, has unfortunately stayed with us till date. No religion ever discriminated against us, history is in our favour and that's just a fact. I made this knowledge my Brahmastra, my lethal weapon, and it has always been part of my activism.

I believe in energies and Mahadev and Shakti have sustained me as an energy source, just as they are inseparable themselves—symbolized in the Ardhanareshwara, which combines the male and female principles—Shiva and Shakti, prakriti and purusha. *Kinnars* (hijras) are worshippers of Shakti, the Goddess, because the mother would never give up the child, no matter what the world thought or said about it. We are part of the Mahadev *kutumb* because it is said in Hindu culture that whoever was rejected by Daksha Prajapati— whoever he thought was a misfit in society—sought shelter with Mahadev, who did not believe in any system. And that's why he has *daanavs*, *pishachinis*, *bhoots*—all the outcasts—everyone under him. They all comprise the wedding procession, his *baraat*, when he goes to wed Parvati. Of course kinnars were a legitimate part of society then, but today, since we are the biggest social outcasts, why not be under him?

I think I have always had a connection with Mahadev. As a child, maybe when I was ten or so, during Mahashivratri, I went and made him my husband. I had kept money aside for a *mangalsutra*, which I bought from the shop myself. And then I went to the temple, clanking my heels, wore the mangalsutra in front of him, and declared to him that we were now married and he was my husband forever; he was my caretaker, and I was under his divine protection. I still remember how the women in the temple went crazy seeing me with my mangalsutra, and hearing me say that I was married to him! For years after that, I would tell anyone and everyone who was interested or not that Shiva is my husband! In a way, I initiated myself as a devadasi then!

The Sole Refuge of Mortals/The Protector

If we are lucky, we have guardian angels in our lives. Darhi wale bhaiyya was one such in mine. His real name was Vijay Pratap Dubey, but we would call him 'Darhi wale bhaiyya' because he kept a beard. He was my *mausi*'s son, and lived with us. In a way, the moment I was born, I was almost placed in his lap. He would take us to school and he would bring our tiffins in the lunch break. As the oldest cousin around, he became a protector of sorts for us children. As a little child, when I lay in bed for days, sick, he would always stay by my bedside, chatting with me, listening to my non-stop chattering, carefully monitoring my medicines and dosage times. I think somewhere he decided to become my 'in-charge' so to speak because he understood that I was different and had a kind of a 'problem'. He realized that I needed protection in the world, *from* this world. And so he always looked out for me.

Darhi wale bhaiyya died of jaundice—how I cried! In his own way, he understood me, and his passing was too great a personal loss for me.

Praveen Balaya is my *bachpan ka dost*, my best friend from the time we were eight or nine years old. We went to different schools, but lived in the same neighbourhood. His father ran a tailoring and stitching shop and my father would frequent it often to get his clothes stitched. That made us family friends as well. We were very close; Praveen even travelled with us to our village for my sister's wedding when we were about fifteen.

Praveen is my companion from that period of my life when I had no respectability in anyone's eyes and nobody understood me. I felt clueless because even I didn't know what I was going through. I had practically no self-respect then because I simply did not understand what to do with my life and my feelings. Every day I would grapple with questions like 'Will everyone disown me?', 'Will I have to become a sex worker?', 'Is my fate sealed?', 'Should I just kill myself?' I did not know who all in my life I could call mine, who would stand by me no matter what. Praveen gave me that assurance just by always being there and by being himself. He could sense that I was different from the other boys because I was so feminine and even had certain 'feminine' interests, which he still remembers! But he never looked at me or thought of me as *ajeeb*, odd. He has always known me this way and he has never questioned it. I've been speaking in a certain way since I was a young boy, often referring to myself as a girl—*Main aa rahi hoon* or *Main jaa rahi hoon*—so he's also become used to it, I guess. When I decided to join the hijra clan later in life, Praveen just said, 'You were, you are, and you will always remain Laxmi for me.' He's always been accepting of me, my tastes and preferences.

We're buddies—he knows me inside out, left, right and centre. If I have a look on my face, any look, he knows exactly what it means. He lost his father at a very young age and then his mother when we were in class ten, so in a way, I became his family. Sometimes I feel like I'm both mother and father to him, as well as a friend. I am a mother to many people, some my age, some even older than me—I don't know why but many people find something maternal in me; it's amazing. It's also a funny relationship—when you go from being friends to being like a mother, but I just love Praveen. When he is ill, I'm the first one to go to him and take him to the doctor. I even insist on his moving in with me so that my chelas can take proper care of him, and make sure he's taking his medicines.

We've had such fun throughout our growing-up years, all those childish pranks and moments of absolute delight that we've shared together. Going to Anthony's Bakery, with Shashi trailing along, and gorging on the delicious pastries. When all of us started drinking and Praveen wouldn't booze, I would mix alcohol in his soft drinks at parties. Having those silly fights—I remember this one time when we had an algebra exam back in class ten. I had borrowed his notes and I forgot to return them because, as always, I was freaking out with the boys while Praveen was getting anxious. We quarrelled about it so much that I ended up tearing those notes in front of him and throwing them at him! We would set out for our class ten tuitions together, but I'd bunk the class because I was too busy hanging out with Nilesh (my then boyfriend) and making out with him everywhere, I was so crazy about him. The teacher would always scream at me, and Praveen would tell me not to act that way. But I couldn't help it!

Now that we've become grown-ups, I find that I'm the submissive one, because I'm slightly frightened of him. He can be so very nasty to me—you know how it is when you grow up with someone, they know how to push your buttons. He's very sweet, but if he's angry with me, he'll fight with my like crazy, insult me and really upset me, making me miserable. Once, he'd asked me to attend the marriage of one of his students—he's a teacher and takes tuitions—so I went. Now, I'm very uncomfortable eating in public, because everybody looks at you and your face doesn't look good while eating—nobody's does! And all those photos they take when you're eating at weddings—very annoying! So I stayed for a while and then left without eating. And the way Praveen fought with me about it! He was furious!

But if he does something similar to me, then I dare not fight with him. I'd once organized a birthday party for him and after the cake was cut and we all sat drinking together, Praveen left without informing anyone—he left his own party! But I didn't fight with him about that, I didn't have the guts. If he feels I'm neglecting him, or if I'm too busy and I haven't called him back, then he'll make sure to screw my happiness. Nobody else in my life would dare do that to me! And after all that, I am the one who has to make up. Each and every time, I'm the one apologizing to and pleading with him! We've had loads of fun at my birthday parties—I haven't had any since Papa passed away, but when we used to have them,

Praveen would wait eagerly for 13 December, deciding which jacket he'd wear and stuff like that.

When we were kids, I was vilified very often because I was different. Almost every day of my life I was made fun of by someone or the other and when you're a child, it can really get under your skin. Today, I am an adult and I have been formed and shaped as an individual with a lot of self-confidence and awareness, but back then, I was like any other child who needed encouragement and support, not abuse and mockery all the time. When I went to Praveen's house wearing my bangles, his mother would scold me and tell me to behave properly, which meant like a 'boy', of course, but Praveen always stood up for me.

By the time we were fifteen, I had managed to instil a lot of attitude in myself, in order to give it back to those who would mock me. If anyone said anything to me, I would retort with something even worse. Praveen remembers that time very well too because he was with me through most of it—he calls that phase my 'drastic transformation'. He reminded me of an episode from those days recently, about a boy I used to like and the price he paid for trying to reject me. He was extremely handsome, and we were fooling around without anyone knowing about it. He was hanging out with his friends when we saw each other on the street one day, and I could see that he was trying everything in his power to avoid me. So I walked straight up to him, grasped his chin, looked him right in the eyes and said, 'What happened, darling? Is there a problem? *Bistar pe toh main achchi lagti hoon tujhe* (You seem to like me in bed).' Those were the days when I was perfecting my talent of being blunt and direct, saying it like it is. Another time a young boy was trying to upset me, calling me a hijra. I waved him over, saying, '*Idhar aao, beta,*' and continued, '*tere bolne se mujhe certificate toh nahi milega. Milega kya*? (Will I get a certificate because you call me that? Will I?)' Once, when I went to meet Praveen in his home, he was taking tuitions. As soon as the children saw me, they all started crying, I don't know why, maybe they were frightened. So I called them close and said, 'What happened, dear children? *Main toh aap se achchi lag rahi hoon, achchi dikhti hoon* (I look better than you). Is that why you're crying?'

Praveen has always wanted the best for me. Even in his dislike is hidden great support for me, and if he admonishes me, it's usually with good reason. For instance, he's the one who's always telling me to pay more attention to my activism and not allow myself to be led astray by relationships or family problems. He tells me to do all I can to increase my focus on social work and engage myself in it even more thoroughly. 'Give it more than a hundred per cent, Laxmi,' he tells me. 'Go to the office more often, be more present.' He feels I have the potential and capacity to do more than I am doing right now—and that kind of faith in one's abilities is so precious, it makes one feel special.

I remember taking a stroll somewhere with Praveen a day after the fifth season of *Bigg Boss*, in which I had participated, aired and being accosted by a gentleman who'd recognized me. We were having a nice conversation and I commented on the gentleman's necklace, complimenting him on its beautiful design. Instantly, the man took it off his neck and made me wear it, saying he'd be very happy if I accepted it. It was a *paanch tola* gold chain! Later, Praveen told me that what I have is truly special—a charisma that draws people—and so I should use it for the betterment of the community.

I know that his love and support for me is unconditional and you need that in life. I can talk about anything and everything with Praveen—he knows me so well we can discuss anything.

I befriended Rahul Kale in my schooldays. We met at a party in Koliwada and I was immediately drawn to his too-cool-for-school attitude. He was effeminate like me, but while I was hesitant in those days in expressing myself, he had a no-holds-barred approach. I learnt a lot from him and today I can admit that by imitating his in-your-face sexuality, which he carried with such style and nonchalance and don't-give-a-damn attitude, I gained a lot in terms of my own self-confidence and self-projection. We started hanging out together and went to many parties—he with his over-the-top display of femininity and me getting there. Eventually, we had a falling-out because I discovered that Rahul was involved in illegal activities and had started swindling people at knifepoint as well. But I never let go of that brazenness that he taught me, and which I nurtured in his company. That, and the other perk of spending time with him—I picked up a lot of cool English words and phrases because Rahul was a convent school lad.

I met Kris in Amsterdam at the Netherlands Transgender Film Festival in 2007, where they were screening *Between the Lines*, a film directed by Thomas Wartmann documenting photographer Anita Khemka's work with hijras, in which I play a prominent part. Kris and I were instantly attracted to each other—we both knew it the moment we set eyes on each other. En route to a party, we held hands, and when Kris took a detour to withdraw money from an ATM booth, I went along with him. We stood by a canal for a long time, our hands intertwined, our eyes locked. I remember I was wearing a bright red lehnga-choli with a silk dupatta. It was slightly cold that evening—the result of a light Amsterdam drizzle—and, seeing me visibly uncomfortable, Kris took off his shirt and draped it around my shoulders. My pulse was racing and just as we were about to kiss, Kris asked me, 'You do know about me, Laxmi, don't you?' I think I was in a trance until then, mesmerized by him, absolutely imprisoned by my attraction for him, but his question broke the spell. I noticed his bare chest and the surgical mark in the shape of a T on it, indicating that the breasts had been removed. It suddenly dawned on me that Kris was born a woman and had become a man out of choice. He had even had gender-confirmation surgery done so he could finally be who he felt he was—a man. But somehow, to me, the thought was discomfiting, unnerving. That I was about to kiss a woman, maybe even sleep with a man who used to be a woman—it was a thought I was not comfortable with, and I immediately broke away, disengaging from his embrace. Kris tried hard to convince me. 'Laxmi, please give it a chance. Give it some time and you'll get used to it.' But I simply wasn't up for it. On the day I flew back home, Kris came to see me off at the airport. We hugged and cried, both of us. I felt as if I was abandoning him, but I couldn't get myself to think of Kris as a man. He even followed me back to Mumbai some months later, but I still did not feel ready for him in that sense.

I like to think that I have matured over the years. Now when I think about it, I can see that I had a phobia back then. I know that what I did was not right, the way I felt and thought, and that I treated him unfairly. But I did what I felt. I did not understand his love, and I could only think, 'Oh, but how can this be possible? A woman turning into a man?' Of course that's ridiculous of me! How can I, of all people, think that way? Now I know better and so I feel I'll be able to relate much better to him. In fact trans men are much more than men, they're so manly.

I spoke with Kris recently and he was very excited to hear my voice. I'll probably be visiting Amsterdam soon, so I'd called him up—that's where he lives and we'll meet when I go there.

No man has ever gone out of my life; I try and make sure that I keep my relationships intact. And so it is with

Kris. Though of course I will not be pursuing anything romantically with him, because I'm in a committed relationship now. But I'll stay friends with Kris.

Every desire of your body is holy

I've had many relationships; I've slept with many men—discovering pleasure, sexuality and my body—but never for money or work. I've only slept with a man for pleasure and I always will. I respect my body too much to let it become part of a transaction like that. Not that I think those who do, do not respect their bodies. I wouldn't say that, because I feel *sab apne maap-dand taiyyar karte hain apni zindagi ke liye* (everyone charts out their own parameters and boundaries for life), and it's not my place to comment on anyone like that. Even the Pope has said, 'Who am I to judge?'

I would say most of my relationships, if not all, have been on my terms. I decided for whom I would take my top off, whom I would ask to unclasp and remove my bra, from whose lips would my silicone breasts hang—all those men who were so intoxicated by my femininity that they could not hold even an inch of their manhood. How I made their patriarchy come crawling to me, on its knees, to my doorstep—to be on my satin bedsheet. So many men came and went and only a few touched maybe just the hairs on my skin—and yet they left satisfied. I think it's beautiful to be a woman when you can make a man feel enslaved like that.

I've made love in the oddest and most exciting of places! On planes! In business class, that too. I was sleeping and the man next to me, European I think, he just went nuts seeing me in my sari. He came over and kissed me, so I pulled him over, and we had sex right there on the seat. I've had sex in economy as well—in the bathroom. Once I slept with a crew member on an Emirates flight—they have a cabin to rest in, and that's where we went. Oh, and once in an air taxi from Gorakhpur to Delhi, where they keep the cargo at the back. During descent, I fixed my hair and make-up, and was back in my seat. That night, after his flight, that guy came to my room in Jor Bagh, for more.

Rohan Joshi was my first kiss—the first time I ever enjoyed a proper kiss was with him. I slept with all three brothers, but Rohan was special. He was very handsome; girls would go wild around him, but I managed to snag him. Our sex was very crude the first time, because he was very drunk. I used to play badminton in school and I had just come back from practice when he pulled me into bed. I didn't say no.

After that, we had sex in all sorts of places, including the terrace of the building!

Then there was Nasir—so very handsome with his sturdy build and fair skin. Matheran 1992 will always be our shared memory, because the first time we did it was on a school trip to Matheran in class twelve. With him, it was all about sex. Picnics in the day and fucking at night. I felt very bold in his company; it was as if I was letting go of all the alienation I had ever felt through my discovery of sex and its pleasures. Nasir would also act as my protector in school. If someone teased me during school hours, he would report them to the class teacher. And if I was teased outside school while he was around, he would take it upon himself to beat them.

Among all these men, I'd say Ravi was my first true love. It was love in the garb of brotherhood. For the world, he was my 'brother' because that's the image we presented, but in reality, we were sleeping with each other. I remember having sex with him on his office table. That was amazing. I loved him too; it wasn't simply about sex for me. But then I got him married to my best friend. Actually, that's why I did it, because I loved him so much. See, I wanted the best for him, and I knew we could not be together forever, because I could not give him a family, and he would want that at some point. Also, when you're so young, you feel you know it all, don't you? Back then I thought love meant sacrifice, and if I really loved him, I should let him go and all that jazz! Such a silly thing to think!

Anyway, I set him up with my best friend Nisha— she and I used to talk about him all the time. And they did get married eventually. It's strange but in a way I lost her as a friend after that, because Nisha began to feel insecure when I was around. I feel that because my presentation of womanhood is so strong, girls tend to be jealous of me, especially if their husband or guy is around and is eyeing me, which happens a lot. In Nisha's case, of course, it's also because she knows that Ravi and I have a shared history, so it's understandable that she's insecure around me. But it's quite a common reaction I get from women—they keep asking their men, 'Why are you talking so much to her?' I don't mind though. The bitches are jealous, not my problem.

I'm in touch with Ravi too; I think I communicate with all my exes till date. Once a man is in Laxmi's life, he's never really out of it. We also grow and evolve, don't we? And that's beautiful to reconnect with.

*When you look deeply into somebody's eyes, you are
looking deeply into yourself, and the other person is
looking deeply into the same self, which many-eyed,
as the mask of Vishnu is many-faced, is looking
out everywhere. One energy playing myriads of
different parts.*

Whom do you call when you really need someone? If there is one man in my life who I know will drop everything in an instant and come to help me the moment I call him, it is Dhan Bahadur Chand, or Chand as I call him. We first met on 8 March 2010—he had invited me to a Women's Day function he was organizing on behalf of Global Vision, a cancer organization which he'd just started. My father was suffering from cancer then, and I felt that it was my responsibility to attend.

At the event, we didn't really talk much, but there was a dinner later in the evening for which he'd come to pick me up. I was wearing this very sexy lehnga—with Swarovski crystals and all that—but it was so heavy, like 10 kilograms or something! A lehnga like that, you have to tie it really tightly, and what happened was that it began to come loose during the dinner party and I didn't know how to adjust it. This was at Samudra hotel, next to Sea Queen in Thane, a very famous ladies' bar, and absolutely my hub.

I needed someone to hold it while I tied it properly again. Chand happened to be sitting next to me, so I decided to just ask him. He looked at me for a moment, slightly taken aback, but then he promptly responded— he caught it and I tied it again. I think, in that moment, a bond was formed between us. We laugh about that moment now. After that, Deepak (Salvi, my adopted son) was organizing a show in which Chand was also involved. We would meet almost every other evening to discuss the details, and our relationship was cemented then, and we became very close to each other.

When my father's condition worsened, Chand was someone I could turn to without hesitation, and I did all the time. He was my support when my father died, when he breathed his last. I had to travel so much in those days when Papa was going from bad to worse. I was trying to do so much, earn money, keep my social activism alive, make sure there was enough money for medicines and doctors. It was Chand who stood by my family through that time. I would call him from wherever I was and simply ask, 'Chand, Papa, Mummy?' And he would say, 'I am going there just now, to be with them.' There was a time during my father's treatment when I didn't have money to pay the hospital. It was Rs 80,000. Chand came at once and he deposited it for me. Nobody does that, not even your own kin. It can only be someone with whom you have a cosmic connection.

Ours has always been a platonic relationship. I would have been in his arms in a moment if he had wished it; at the time, all I wanted was for him to take ownership of me. But he was already married with kids when I met him and that has always kept me in check. How could I destroy a marriage, a family? I would lose respect in my own eyes. (Of course some married men are assholes, and then, perhaps, I'm also a super bitch at times. But am I the only one?) Chand is a wonderful man. And he's the only one I can say this about confidently—that if he had owned me, Viki (Thomas) would never have been a part of my life today.

At my father's funeral, I was holding on to Chand and crying the whole time. He stood by me, like a pillar of strength. He even travelled to the village for my father's *tervi*, and brought Deepak along with him. I was trying to be strong for my mother's sake, staying by her side, constantly telling her how important she is to me . . . I was also going through so much pain, thinking about how, after her, there won't be anybody who'll call me and ask me about myself. When Papa was alive, that's what he would do, and with that knowledge, I began to feel paranoid about my mother, because in this world, there is nobody else who cares that much about you, who worries about these things—Are you fine? Did you sleep? Did you eat? Only parents think that way, they are your biggest assets.

There were so many people in the house during the ceremony that we all had to sleep together on mats, next to each other. Chand spent nights like that too—even one's daughter's husband would refuse to sleep like that, but he did it for the two days he was there, like true family. I don't think I can ever compensate him for everything that he has done for me—the time he has given my family, and the situations in which he has stood by them.

I truly believe that somewhere my soul is connected with his. We go for weeks without speaking to each other at times, but somehow, when one of us is really in some kind of pain, or has been recently, we reconnect. The other day when I called him after months, he told me that he was not feeling well, having suffered a bad bout of food poisoning. I'm so sure that that was why the call happened that day—it was meant to be.

❦

Pravin Bera used to live in my area, in Shastri Nagar, Thane (West). He's several years younger than me, and so to me, as I was growing up, he was a baby, really.

Pravin used to be frightened of me, I remember, running away whenever he saw me. My first memories of him are him sitting on his bike in this favourite shirt he wore quite often—plain blue with white checks. I would tease him, referring to him as 'Daddy' for fun, and slowly I think he began to be less frightened of me, and more intrigued, trying to figure out what I was all about! And over a period of time, we became friends. Pravin started his own business, grew in it quite well, and became stable over the years while I went on my own adventures. I've travelled with him through Rajasthan a lot—in Ajmer and Jaipur—and I always book two separate rooms for the both of us, because we share that beautiful platonic love I'd only heard about and have been fortunate enough to have found with him. And perhaps, you could say, with him and him alone. He goes out of the way for me and does everything he can for me, without any agenda—I can buy super-expensive saris when we go out shopping and he won't even bat an eyelid! But it still remains an absolutely pure relationship, which has been rare in my life. Most men help you once or twice and the third time will definitely expect you to bed them. With him, I've never got that vibe because it's never been there.

My brother-in-law, Rukmini's husband and my *jijaji* or *jiju*, has been a very significant presence in my life. He is Wing Commander Jeetendra Dutt Mishra and since army men tend to be quite macho, he and his family did not take very kindly to me initially. My parents were also very anxious about this—one of the constant worries Papa had when I became a hijra was concerning Didi's in-laws and what they would think. Jiju has had a fairly modest upbringing—the kind that most of us have—fulfilling all his responsibilities as a son, getting his sisters married, and so on. There was a time when he was most critical of me. He could never understand the hijrotic issues of my life and it was easier to condemn them as abnormal. But today I would say he is the most sorted person in our family. From being one of my biggest critics, he has become one of the most supportive men of my life, having reached a place where he not only appreciates me for who I am, but also praises me for all that I have achieved and recognizes my sacrifices. He's undergone a complete change of perspective, and I feel that's a very big deal—to come from that patriarchal world and to be able to understand me to that extent is no mean feat. Like everyone else, he started out not wanting to know me at all. But today he not only respects me, but also cares about my well-being, and is constantly looking into that. I know I can count on him as someone who will be there to support me if I need him.

One of the things he loves to say about Rukmini and me is that our genders got mixed up at birth. My sister is just like a man, *poora danger ladka*—she's always been in brawls and fights, is very aggressive, ready to fight and bash up anyone. 'Rukmini should have been born a boy,' Jiju says, 'and you, Laxmi, a girl.'

I have wanted to be a mother ever since I was a child myself. If there is one emotion I knew I wanted to fully understand and experience, it was of motherhood. After I had my revenge for being abused, I think I vented out all the negativity in me; I was content. I was ready to feel the giving and nurturing side of womanhood and so, even though I was very young, I felt I was ready to be a mother. And when the opportunity arose, I took it.

Deepak Salvi came into my life through dance—we were introduced by my friend Sachin Kharat. Deepak was my dance student and he gradually became my dance assistant. He even began to run our little school, which we called Lucky Chap Dance Academy, full-time once I stepped down. I anyway think of my students as my children and I adopted Deepak as my son.

I gave up dance because destiny took me elsewhere, but Deepak still works as a dancer, and organizes events and performances. He always had a sense of ownership about me. He questioned anybody I was dating, and always wanted me to be involved in his life decisions. Like I feel and do for my mother, he does for me.

I got him married. His wife, Megha, thinks of me as her mother-in-law. I'm a strict mother-in-law, I scold her often. On one holy occasion, she was out wearing a sleeveless top—this was after the marriage, and I told her that she shouldn't wear all this in public, especially now that she was married. I would make her understand, 'Bahu, this is not how it works. After marriage, everyone has to make these adjustments. It's not about individuals any more, it's about making families. When you're in a relationship, it's different, but in a marriage, it's complete commitment to family . . .' At times I am taken aback by my own conservatism but life is full of contradictions, isn't it?

Sometimes in relationships, there are cracks, and somehow, that's what happened with Deepak. We have become somewhat distant but neither of us is very sure of the reasons. But Deepak has always been a loving child and I will love him till my last breath. Mothers are mothers!

Uday Anchan is my second son. Uday and I were sworn enemies for very long, we hated each other from the very core of our beings. But then things changed. When his mother was diagnosed with cancer, he called me, and I tried to help him through it. That was our connection. We went to the Sai Baba temple one evening, and just as we were about to enter, he said to me, 'If Deepak can be your son, why can't I?' And I said to him, 'Fine. From today you'll be my son till my last breath.' He lost his mother to the disease eventually and I think I became the motherly figure in his life. I am a very good mother; I let my children do whatever they want. Uday is my cute little baby. He's very handsome and sweet, always working out. He's very religious as well. I've been telling him to get married—'Because mother needs new saris and jewellery!' I say. Sometimes I tell him that if I had the power to make another Uday, I would and I would make that Uday my husband!

Uday's birthday is on the same day that I lost my father—8 August—and for some reason, I have always thought that when my father's body was being taken for the funeral, *jab kandha de rahe the*, he was standing right there. In my memory, he's there, but he tells me he wasn't. I have asked him so many times, 'You were there, weren't you, *beta*?', and he always gives me the same answer, '*Nahi maate*, I was not there.' He always calls me *maate*, as do all his friends. I just love hearing it!

I now believe it was my father in his disguise, standing there and watching what was happening. Souls don't go away, and your parents' souls especially are always with you. In my mind, on that day, his soul had taken Uday's form.

Prince Manvendra Singh Gohil of Rajpipla in Gujarat is the first member of Indian royalty to come out as openly gay. But that's too simple a statement for it does not take into account many painful facts concerning his background, a lifetime of denial, hurt, anger, confusion that ended in a nervous breakdown. When you're royalty, people believe it's an enviable life because you're always in the lap of luxury. While this might be true, what nobody talks about is that you have practically no freedom. And freedom of expression is not a birthright. Growing up as the heir apparent of Rajpipla, Manvendra led an intensely protected life, closeted from the outside world—with no awareness of homosexuality or what being gay meant, he spent years wondering if he would ever become 'normal'—that is, not be attracted to members of his own sex—again.

Following a script already written for him, as is customary when you're born into a royal family, he was married to Princess Chandrika Kumari of Jhabua, Madhya Pradesh, when his parents thought it time. And the prince himself was certain the marriage would 'cure' him and soon there would be progeny to prove it too. But it was an unhappy marriage, with, as the prince puts it, 'two miserable people, instead of just one'. The marriage, unconsummated, ended a year later in divorce and caused much bitterness, especially for Manvendra's parents. There was more talk of marriage, but the prince refused, though he still kept his true feelings hidden.

In 2002, the prince suffered a nervous breakdown and started undergoing counselling. Even though the psychiatrists informed his parents, the king and queen, of their son's sexual orientation, they kept it a secret and pressured Manvendra to do the same. But finally in 2006, at the age of forty-one, Manvendra came out to the world, deliberately choosing a Gujarati language newspaper to make the declaration. The king and queen were devastated and the queen issued a full-page announcement in the newspaper saying that Prince

Manvendra had been disowned. Shunned by his own family, the prince continued to maintain that he would stand by his truth. 'I knew they would never accept me for who I truly am, but I also knew that I could no longer live a lie,' he told Oprah Winfrey in a 2007 appearance. (He was invited back to the famous show in 2011.)

Determined to work towards the eradication of the social stigma around homosexuality in India, Manvendra started his own charitable organization, the Lakshya Trust, and has been working tirelessly on the issues concerning the gay community ever since.

He is like my soulmate; I am a sister to him. Our relationship is that of a real brother and sister, even more than my own blood brother. He's given me the true happiness of having a brother I can depend on and love, one who loves me back deeply.

We became close when we encountered each other at the National Aids Control Society meeting in Mumbai though we had met prior to that. But I didn't know then that he was a prince. He had absolutely no airs about him, he was so grounded and humble, and it was clear that he was there to work. Of course, as I got to know him, I understood that this is who he is—he's just a very special and down-to-earth gentleman, with no chip on his shoulder about being royalty.

Our connection was instant, one of those very rare and special bonds you're lucky to make in life at times. And we began to relate as brother and sister. He always calls me for his birthday celebrations at the palace—there's always a concert and several events around it—so whenever I am free, I do go and attend them. The first time I went, even though I had never stayed in a royal palace before, I didn't feel out of place even once. He introduced me as his sister everywhere, to everyone. Now the entire city treats me like his sister. In fact, he jokingly said to the press that we had separated at the Kumbh Mela when we were kids and that we'd found each other now—they actually printed that as a fact and till date, I am asked to clarify it! But in a way, that's exactly how we feel—that perhaps we were separated—and that's why we came close to each other. Whenever I have an important event in my life, I call him, and he's always there. I'll never forget how, when I lost my father, he came to attend the funeral, driving all the way from Rajpipla. *(Turn to page 123, for 'Prince Manvendra's Monologue: Laxmi, My Sister')*

When you face serious discrimination, you have to be strong, and along the way you come across a few caretaker angels who help you strengthen your cause and fight for it, right by your side. My friend Anand Grover of the Lawyers' Collective is one such person. He supported me through the ordeal when I was thrown out from a dinner party I was attending as a delegate at a sexuality conference in Bombay Gymkhana. I was appalled and humiliated. I hadn't even finished eating, but no concessions were allowed. Most importantly though, I was extremely angered by it—by what it means for the movement if a well-known activist is thrown out of so-called mainstream, progressive and elite places. It simply means we can never be accepted. It shows the hangover of India's upper class. And, its double standards. It was then that I sought Anand's support and help, and with him on my side, I sent the club a legal notice. I demanded a public apology from the club and from the CEO, Brigadier R.K. Bose, who had interrupted the dinner party and asked my hosts, Ajay and Parvesh, to tell me to leave. I still remember Ajay's face as he approached me, relaying the information he'd just received, tears welling up in his eyes. The case was admitted on grounds of discriminatory behaviour, and it was a strong case, but somewhere down the line I lost interest in pursuing it and decided not to fight it. I just put the matter behind me, choosing to focus instead on the bigger battles. But

Anand's support through that episode is something I will never forget.

Anand has been a passionate supporter of the LGBT movement and has always been appreciative of my work. If the NALSA judgement was declared in our favour, and there was finally an acknowledgement of the third gender, it was all because of Anand. That day— 15 April 2014—will remain etched in my mind forever, and in the minds of so many hijras who, until then, had been made to feel that they had no existence, who were denied dignity in life, and in death. When a hijra dies, we wait for dusk, for everyone to fall asleep. Then we steal through the night like thieves to offer last rites to our comrades, escaping everyone's attention. Was this life? Or mere existence? The landmark judgement—a golden moment for us—is an acceptance of our sexuality in the eyes of the law and that is a huge step forward in the right direction. That transgenders can live with dignity, something that each and every human being is entitled to, *should* be entitled to, is something we've all been fighting for.

That day, after the verdict was announced, we were all dancing together at Jantar Mantar in New Delhi—the air was electric, full of cheer and laughter. I remember joking around with the crowd that Anand

was my boyfriend! Interestingly, after the verdict, a
transgender law student who had dropped out in the
second year called to inform me that she was getting
enrolled again to complete her studies. It is things like
this that make it all worth it. Nobody is interested in
giving you your rights. It is up to you to take them.
How to use the law depends on the individual and,
until that moment, I always say, we had waited for
more than two centuries for justice. And of course, it
needs to be ensured, to some extent, that the ruling is
implemented properly. We know that Tamil Nadu and
Maharashtra have already constituted the Transgender
Welfare Board, and other states too have started taking
requisite measures. A number of welfare programmes
have been set up to sensitize those implementing the
law, because sensitization, as we know, is crucial.
Several bureaucrats and police officers at the Centre
have been extremely supportive about the judgement
and what it means, and its execution. Anand has been
crucial for all of it. He's such a well-respected and
amazing lawyer, and extremely helpful. If, at any time
in my life, I ever need legal help or assistance of any
kind, I know he'll be there for me. He's a true believer
in the cause and, what I find humbling, in my abilities
to represent hijras. Even in the Supreme Court, he

presented the Section 377 case in a beautiful way. I have very high regard for him.

Sometimes in life you forge deep bonds in the most unexpected of places! I met someone who went on to become a dear friend at a beauty pageant in Chennai, which I also, incidentally, won! Pradeep Kattikal was running an organization then that had worked on the event and we got to know each other and became friends during that time.

I remember I got an asthma attack because of the heat there and Pradeep took me to the doctor and took such good care of me. He's a very handsome Malayali guy and I think I began to nurse a serious crush on him! Pradeep went on to rise in the world and gained status— he started working with the UNAIDS and today, he is the political advisor to the UNAIDS Executive Director's office in Geneva. I respect his position and how hard he's worked for it and I think it's a mutual feeling, because he too has seen me really grow from the Laxmi I was to the Laxmi I have become. I met him in June 2016 at the UN High Level Meeting in New York, and there too, he was taking care of me. I can say that with him, it's an evolution—from just a crush, he became a friend and today, I can say he's like family. I often find myself taking his advice and following his directions, because he's a very sensible guy.

Pawan came into my life in 2007. We met at the Infosem conference in Juhu. At first, I don't think he liked me—the way hijras behave with their big bindis and the aggression alienated him. At that time, it was all about identity, and in order to distinguish ourselves from the MSM group, we transgenders had to be loud and make sure we were noticed. Pawan was a lost soul then, struggling with several issues, and conflicted in his sexuality—he grew up in a very conservative environment in his home town, Amravati, attracted to men and feeling helpless. He was devastated when I met him, almost suicidal. He used to be part of an organization called Sarthi then and he invited me as a chief guest for an event. There was a fashion show at the event, where Pawan dressed in drag for the first time, and we had a lot of fun together. If you ask him, he'll tell you that the one thing I know how to do, or at least knew how to do once, is have fun—absolute *dhamaal*! He came to live with us in my house in Thane for a few days and I think that's when our attachment really deepened, as it does when people live together. In those days, I had an Umrao Jaan stance and aura—I would hold court in a way, posing with my hookah—it was a lot of fun. He started calling me his guru and shared all his problems with me, hoping that I could help him solve them. What was going to be a three-day stay turned into months and then years. He shifted base to Mumbai and moved in with us. In 2013, we conducted the ritual to initiate him into the hijra community, and did his *haldi-kumkum*. He's been with me ever since, as my chela.

One day, he was feeling frustrated and he came to me and said, 'You're not helping me with anything.' So I said, 'Let's go now.' Together, we went and registered a new organization in his name, Samarpan Trust, got him the certification and all the official documents and everything. Samarpan gave him a purpose and drive in his life. Now Pawan runs several projects, like the Pehchaan project that's currently under way in association with the Maharashtra Youth Control Society. He's also the director of two more organizations, one in Nagpur and one in Thane.

The beauty of my relationship with Pawan is that even when I'm completely silent, and we're not saying anything at all to each other, we understand each other perfectly. Pawan has seen so many phases of my life—he's supported me in my worst moments and joined me in celebrating the best. He's one of those few people with whom I feel very strongly about having a past-life link. And it's a commitment for life—I won't leave him until his last breath, and he won't until mine—we know that for sure. When he's away, I feel an incompleteness within me.

The way Pawan has respected and maintained all his ties and relationships is amazing. He balances everything very beautifully, be it his own biological family or this, his adopted family, which is our family. In his biological family, he was always the unwanted child whom nobody understood; no one even tried. From being that to becoming a responsible member of the family, someone who has taken on the responsibility of his *bhabhi* after her husband, his brother, died—he's come a long way. In my own family, I can easily say he is like the common thread that binds me to everyone. He also manages so many moods and people at home—no mean feat given all the different temperaments and personalities in my house!

Pawan is extremely sensitive and though he can never express his own feelings, he lets us know how he feels in his own way. When my chela Shaheen was suffering from AIDS, Pawan took excellent care of her, he did everything possible for her. As far as I'm concerned, I know that if Pawan is around, I can relax—he will find a way to get things done. My other chelas became jealous of him, and tried to rile him up, saying that I take him with me for international conferences because 'Laxmi needs someone to carry her bag'. They taunt him about how he can never be a true hijra because he doesn't always don saris, and he doesn't know how to clap properly like a hijra. But he takes it all in his stride.

I believe that everyone gains importance by their deeds, and Pawan has proved himself repeatedly. To me, love is not about saying 'I love you'; it is a person's actions, their deeds that say 'I love you'.

I clarified an important point for his benefit at a public event—that a hijra isn't a hijra because of the clothes she wears; it is her soul that is hijra. I wear a sari because I love saris, I just love them. But Pawan can wear a shirt and trousers, or keep a beard, or whatever he wants—he will always be a hijra. I clarified this in a strong statement at the event and that was important to Pawan, because when your guru acknowledges it in public, it cannot be questioned by anyone else.

When Pawan was initiated into the hijra community, he asked me what name he should take on. For me, the soul matters and Pawan, I know, has a very pure soul. So I said he should be named Pavitra. And he is Pavitra today. When he asks me why our paths didn't cross earlier in life and says that if they had, he would've been an 'original hijra', I tell him, 'Please. You are Hijra No. 1! You are Pavitra. Don't let anyone tell you otherwise.'

If Pavitra is my chela, Jumman is my hijra soul. The foremost chela of renowned hijra guru Raji Haji of Pathankot, Jumman is very famous herself, and known in our community as BBC because of how well connected she is and for the speed with which she can relay any news concerning the hijra community, especially in north India, where she has a special foothold. She's like a one-stop shop for anything and everything there is to know about the hijra world in India—every single hijra, every guru, the details of the workings of each and every gharana, and of course countless secrets that lie buried in her chest. Initially I was hesitant about befriending her, or even approaching her, because I was worried about what she might think of me and the kind of things she might say to the rest of the community. Jumman made several attempts to reach out to me. Once, she even came home and brought me a gift of seven saris, but I had to rush off somewhere and couldn't really sit and entertain her. After we became friends, she told me how much that angered her. She thought I was giving her attitude for no reason. 'You just put on your lipstick and left, so I thought you were very arrogant,' she said. 'Of course I had no idea then that you were a celebrity and that every moment of your time is precious.' Now that we're friends, we get along like a house on fire!

With Jumman by my side, I can walk into any hijra's house without even thinking twice, and I know there'll be nothing but the best kind of hospitality awaiting us. We are inseparable now and when we're together, we go crazy laughing and talking, especially because Jumman is full of hilarious stories and episodes and is an excellent mimic! She's also a huge Bollywood fan and has met some 3000-odd actors, as she likes to say, and has a plethora of stories about every celebrity! She's a huge Salman Khan fan and has created many a scene outside his apartment complex after getting drunk. (Of course I promptly get a call from the security, asking me to handle the matter!)

Because of the severe politics in our community, there have been several episodes of people trying to create rifts between us. We've had terrible fights as a result, to the point where we even resorted to trying to harm each other physically. But then the next day, all was well again and we were back together.

If there are any decisions I need to take with regard to my community, I never take them without consulting Jumman first. She has always guided me in these matters, helping me understand what is right, what is wrong, all the while keeping my best interests in mind. In all these years, she has never misused me or exploited my status as a celebrity, which people frequently try to do. So I have great respect for her. I became Laxmi guru's chela, a famous hijra guru in Delhi, who's popularly known as Doctorni—and she disowned me because she didn't approve of my ways and my lifestyle. Some time later, she called me back and said she wanted me to become her chela again. When I consulted Jumman, she told me not to do that. She told me that it wasn't a decision to be made lightly; we would have to think it through because my guru couldn't be someone who would impose restrictions on me—I can never give up my freedom. My guru needs to be fine with the fact that I travel a lot because it's part of my work. So she told me not to act on it for the moment, and I'm following her advice.

Jumman was very close to her mother, and was grief-stricken when she lost her to a brain haemorrhage. She

LAXMI

had even got married like a regular man for her mother's happiness. Jumman—whose real name is Sayeed Ahmed; his nickname came from the movie *Mehboob ki Mehndi*—is a father to four lovely children, and he is wonderful with them.

They say that hijras bond through pain, their ties are forged in pain and suffering, and that's how our relationship has developed too, I feel.

And I have my hijra sisters too—I call them both my *behen*—Kamini and Muskaan. I've known Kamini for nineteen years; she is my absolute best friend in the community. I can share anything and everything with her. I met Muskaan through Kamini—I remember she was wearing a brown Punjabi suit with a silver lace border and she was looking so beautiful when we first met. She has these beautiful *nasheeli ankhen* (sexy eyes) that drew me to her.

Both of them have stood by me in a very tough time—when I came out of the *Bigg Boss* house, there were death threats issued against me by the community, because according to their rigid rules, I had done something unforgivable by appearing in a TV show. So I ran to Delhi and lived with Muskaan and Kamini, both of whom were very insistent that I live with them.

They joined me for the Ujjain Kumbh in June 2016 and stayed there with me for a month and a half, without even bothering to think about what the community might do, or what kind of action might be taken against them. And neither want any formal positions, they just want to be there with me. We had such fun together in Ujjain—Kamini was sitting on a horse and somehow still managing to dance for six hours straight! And when the cottage that was given to me as the Acharya Mahamandaleshwara of the kinnar akhara—my new position—became slightly muddy because of the rains, I asked them both to shift to the ashram, but they wouldn't hear of it! 'We'll stay with you, no matter what the conditions are!' they said. I was so touched by that.

Our souls have past-life connections I'm quite certain—when there is unspoken dialogue, and only eye contact is needed to communicate, you can be sure that it's a past-life connection.

Vijay Nair, who is affectionately called Goda or Goda bai, was the person who welcomed me into the new world of queer identities and made me feel accepted through the ritual of haldi-kumkum. This was back in 1997 when I had gone to meet Ashok Row Kavi at Maheshwari Gardens. I was so very young then and absolutely disoriented. I would often go with my school bag to meet them. I wanted to become a part of their group because I thought they were my people and that they would understand me. I was desperately searching for an identity to call my own, to feel that sense of belonging—everyone needs it, and I never really had it.

Goda would really discourage me at first. 'You're so very young, just a child,' she would say. 'Do your homework and don't think about all this.' It was later that I understood she was trying to protect me from making any rash choices. As an older person, she thought it her duty to give me the right advice. So she would advise against it. Back then, it was also a very dangerous decision and she had experienced all the consequences first-hand. Just like me, she had faced confusion and ostracism, especially during school. In those days it was not easy for gay men to meet even in parks, as consenting adults—they were constantly being harassed by cops, the moral policing *sevak* kinds, who were really just goons. They often had to face threats of physical violence, and were beaten up quite regularly because of their professed sexual orientations. They were all trying to shield me from this pain and torture, particularly Goda, because she could see that I was effeminate like her. She would keep trying to nudge me away from this world, telling me that if I had even the faintest options of not choosing this life, then I must take it. 'Choosing this life path is a very difficult decision,' she cautioned, 'and one should only make this decision if there is absolutely no other choice available.' She told me, again and again, that it just wasn't the right place for me—that it wasn't right for me, that I was extremely young, and that I should just go and study. 'Education is important—concentrate on that.'

But have I ever listened to anyone but myself?

I was completely drawn towards them, and then I felt very strongly that this was where I belonged. Goda remembers even today how I was absolutely adamant and very certain about it. 'You were stubborn, Laxmi— you always have been,' she says. 'Once you've made up your mind about something, you'll see through it, I know. You have a strong mental disposition.' I was quite sure even then that I would prevail on her. Whenever I met her, I would touch her feet and say *'paon padti'*— that by touching her feet, I'm requesting her to bless me and adopt me as one of her own, as one of her children.

I was very persistent about being part of the community. She had no option but to give in. One fine day, she finally acknowledged me as one of her own, and you know what she did? She took me in her arms, she took the sands of Maheshwari Gardens, smeared my forehead with it and told me, 'This girl is Miss Thane. From today, she's christened as Miss Thane and this is your haldi-kumkum ceremony.' That was a very emotional moment for both of us, whether we realized it then or not. It definitely created a bond between us, an everlasting bond.

I believe that moment marked the turning point of my life in a way, because I became reasonably comfortable in my skin. Being accepted by the elders of the community gave me immense self-confidence and a tremendous sense of entitlement. Even though I was still not very sorted about who I was in that sense, and some confusion about myself, my identity remained, I began to feel like I was part of something, which comes with the sense of belonging and ownership in a community.

Goda has seen me transform over the years, as I transitioned through several identities. Initially I aligned myself with the kotis—Goda identified herself as a koti, who are effeminate men, and face a lot of stigma even within the gay community. Especially in those days, gay men were not supposed to be effeminate; because they were men who liked to have sex with other men, they had to have an aggression about them. Goda was always looking out for me, and she would warn me: 'Think about your decision, Laxmi. Being a koti is very tough.' Then I moved on to identify myself with hard-core gay men. That was a time when we didn't really speak much, because gay men wouldn't interact too much with other kotis. We had more of a hi-bye equation then, Goda and I, because as a hard-core gay man, you would never want to be even seen talking to a koti. After many, many years, Goda saw me being extremely effeminate again, and becoming more aligned with the identity of a transgender person, a transgender woman. And then, of course, I finally became hijra—within the hijra community is where I found the greatest self-alignment and self-identification. And till date, that's how I see myself—as hijra.

Over the years, whenever we meet or speak, I always say '*paon padti Goda bai*' to her—it's like I've made her my mother in a way, it's how I feel about and relate to her. Kotis normally have a mother–sister relationship with others in the community, and men who identify themselves as kotis always have a feminine name. Hers being Goda, short for Godavari, and when I call her that, it's with a lot of endearment and affection. Otherwise I just call her Amma. I could be a prominent leader for others, but to her, I'm a child and she's my Amma, my Goda bai. In the hijra community, we have gurus, but a mother is different, and a guru is different. There will always be pure love in a mother–daughter relationship and that's what we have on a personal level. I'm also extremely well received by her biological family—Goda's own mother especially is very fond of me.

We also relate exceptionally well on the professional level; it's a very productive relationship, in that sense. Goda has also achieved quite a lot, initially at the Humsafar Trust in times when they would never let anyone get ahead, and now at the India HIV/AIDS Alliance. She has also started her own organization, Udaan, which works with sexually marginalized groups with a focus on HIV/AIDS. If she needs me for anything, I'm right there by her side. If something major is happening at the policy level, I always call and solicit her advice, discussing how the facts and facets of a particular point should be presented. Since I am now a familiar face in the social development sector and everyone has come across my persona, I have a large network that I can tap into, so she'll ask for my help on that front. Goda always tells me that she finds me special because of the way I conduct my activism. 'It's one of the greatest aspects of Laxmi,' she says. 'She has always fought for everyone—anyone and everyone who is marginalized in our society, especially the sexual minorities, will find a spokesperson in Laxmi. It's not only transgendered people that she's concerned with, but she's also involved with rights for the gay community at large. She fights equally hard for Section 377, which directly affects the gay community. Even though she's part of the hijra community, Laxmi has always supported the rights of all sexual minorities.' Goda understands the landscape of the social sector and its intense politics when it comes to sexual minorities. It's almost an unwritten rule that if you belong to one sector, you can't possibly care for other sector and fight for any rights. It's all very exclusive and divisive—us and them. It is very silly, and I have never cared for all that. If I want to fight for something, I will—I don't care about the ugly politics. 'Politics apart, be it hijras, gays or kotis, Laxmi believes in a larger cause and she is always there for everyone,' Goda says. I have always supported the koti community even more so because I feel they need more support. Kotis are generally lower-middle-class men who have been forcibly married—they need their family structures, they cannot completely do without them. So they have their male partners on the one hand and their wives on the other; both their families and their community. 'Laxmi, you are one of the very few people who have been able to understand this properly,'

Goda says to me, because I stand by her and kotis, whom she represents. 'Even Ashok has never stood by us kotis the way that you have, since he has always identified only with the gay men movement,' she tells me.

Goda loves my forthrightness. In the initial years, when the Gay Pride parade had just started, the so-called big leaders of the gay community would participate in it, but they would all wear masks because they were not comfortable revealing their identities. Maybe because they feared the backlash, or perhaps it was too big a step to take for them. Goda has never taken part herself in the parade, but she is always happy to see me lead it. When I'm in the parade, I'm open about it, making speeches and proclaiming my queer status loud and clear. So Goda says to me, 'You've never needed masks because you have never had anything to hide. You were very bold and open even when you were young. When we'd met for the first time too, you were ready to fight, you would never give up what you considered your rights. And it is this immense boldness and strength of character and mind that makes you the amazing and powerful leader you are today, Laxmi.' Goda appreciates and encourages me when I take any initiative. When I was nominated to the CCM of the Global Fund, she voted for me—and it was a clean sweep in my favour because of the faith that Goda and people like her placed in me. She admires my standing up for everyone. She knows for a fact that it's not easy to be in the hijra community and work with other sexual minorities—hijras have their own gharanas and havelis and rules and codes of conduct and so many dos and don'ts—but it's all about working towards a common end. And with the hijras too, I'm trying to modernize and rectify what I think needs repair in the ways of the community. I'm not fine just with being a celebrity hijra, the popularity means nothing if you don't live up to why you're doing what you're doing. There are issues that I want to talk about, I'm looking to create more awareness and greater acceptance, make a strong impact. So of course I'll talk about all issues—concerning HIV policies, gay men, injecting drug users, everyone. 'That's exactly what one needs to see and should see in a leader. Someone who can take all the issues and is both willing and able to present them at the national and international level,' Goda often says.

I remember we were at an international conference in Korea together, where I was advocating for the rights of Korean sex workers. At one point during the protest, we saw the police marching towards us to shut us down, but we did not waver. When we came back, Goda told me how feats like that make a person a leader, how I am a natural leader and a born fighter. She's always telling people in her community to try and learn from me, especially what she calls my 'brilliant strategizing and relationship-building skills'. I always reply, 'Amma, I'm just talking, speaking my mind. What strategy!' If I am conversing with Muslim leaders, then I'll talk in chaste Urdu, obviously, and discuss the Quran. When I interact with Hindu leaders, the Bhagavad Gita is my reference point. If I'm meeting Rahul and Sonia Gandhi, or Devendra and Amruta Fadnavis (the chief minister of Maharashtra and his wife), then of course one has to speak in a certain manner acceptable in diplomatic and political circles. When Goda commends my skills and achievements, I always say, '*Arre Amma, tumhare se hi seekhi hoon* (I have learnt it all from you).' But she holds firm, adding that no, it's something that *she* needs to learn from me and how she's still learning.

Another time, we were at a conference in Delhi where Swami Agnivesh began saying some controversial things about sexual minorities. When I started talking, I think I took a somewhat aggressive approach, and was partly attacking what had been said. It was Goda bai who gestured to me, telling me to temper it down. One cue from her and I started toning it down and tried to do damage control.

The result was a standing ovation for me. As soon as I stepped off the stage, I asked her, '*Maine kiya na balance, Amma* (Did I manage to balance it well)?' Sometimes she'll get angry with me and scold me, '*Tu bahut zyaada boli aaj* (You went overboard today),' and then I'll say, '*Yeh toh meri quality hai, Amma, de jitni gaali deni hai* (Curse me all you want, but that's my strong point).' Sometimes the fact that I can get quite loud-mouthed and fiery upsets her. She'll tell me that it's a bit extreme, and that I shouldn't be such a *munhphat* and say something incendiary. At times she'll pick up the phone and call me and say to me, '*Aisa nahi bolna chahiye tha, Laxmi* (You shouldn't have said all that). They're powerful people.' And I'll try to reassure her, '*Nahi, Amma, koi baat nahi. Hum kum powerful hain kya?*' I also reason it out with her, '*Galat bola na, Amma, unhone, aisa nahi chalta hai* (They spoke wrongly, that's not fine).' Then she'll mellow down and say to me, 'But Laxmi, you're a national leader, you need to balance it. Be careful, baba.'

Goda really likes that I am still with my family; she always says that family *ko pakad ke rakhna* is a great strength of mine. That both my biological family and my community family are dear to me and that we all stay together is something she loves about me. She sees that as a particular strength of mine, since it's not easy keeping both close to each other. But I have good equations with haveli hijras and equally strong equations with those outside the fold also.

Goda likes to cite me and my story as an example when she speaks with the community. 'It's almost impossible for a hijra to come up in life like that, and to be able to do that with your family bonds strongly in place is unbelievable, but Laxmi has done it,' she tells them. 'Laxmi has got so many hijra leaders coming out and talking about our issues and talking so well. Acceptance is a long way off for any of us, we know that—especially in a culture and country like ours, but Laxmi will surely play a strong and prominent role in shaping the future of queer identities.' She likes to talk about the advocacy of the NALSA judgement and tells the community, '*Laxmi ban gaye toh lottery lag gayi* (If you become Laxmi, it's like you've won the lottery), so you must all try.' One day she calls me up and tells me, pride in her voice, 'From the confused Laxmi to the confident Laxmi, I have really seen you evolve and go from strength to strength.' And some days, Goda bai will say to me, 'Everybody cannot be Laxmi, because Laxmi is in her own league. Am I right, Laxmi?' And I'll laugh and respond, 'Yes, Amma'.

I have known Ganesh Sawant aka Gauri from those Maheshwari Gardens days of being gay, since 1994 or so, and we've been more than friends ever since, more like siblings. We would meet at Maheshwari Gardens every Sunday and if we had money and were feeling rich, we would go off to Vajreshwari where a lot of gay men came in drag. We would wear saris there. Ganesh, being part of a typical orthodox Maharashtrian family, would lie at home and say he was going to a puja or a party and steal his sister's blouse and his mother's sari.

He lived in Malad and I was in Thane, so we met at Dadar station almost every day on our way to college. Often, however, he would pretend not to know me and try and dissociate himself from me. He would even ask me to stay away from him. I was bewildered by his behaviour at first, but of course, gradually I realized that he was struggling with his own sexuality and identity, and given his family background and the fact that his father was an assistant commissioner of police, it was quite tough for him. I used to be ultra-feminine in those days—I always describe myself as a bottle of Pepsi that goes *shizz* when you shake it. My femininity poured out of me unchecked and a lot of people wanted to step away from that shizz! With my fake nails and bindis and long hair, I would never hide who I was, but for someone like him, going through what he was, seeing me like that must have been an uncomfortable experience. I remember I would land up at his college, Ruparel College, if we hadn't met for many weeks, and he would run off and hide in the Arts building to avoid meeting me!

Over time, as he started gaining confidence about himself and his sexuality, we hung out a lot—I think my influence also rubbed off on him and helped him on his journey. Also because of the way I was then—tall, loud, bindaas, over the top, posturing with my femininity, big talker—there were always plenty of boys around me. And though I was the one who stood out, Ganesh—who was otherwise shy and self-effacing, still coming to terms with his sexuality and not comfortable expressing it— got access to them as well. That was an added advantage for him and also helped him evolve, I feel.

I remember there was a Holi trip planned to Danapani, part of the Aksa beach, and it was to be a major LGBT bash. It was all about colourful, intoxicating and wild fun. I was late reaching the station, which was the rendezvous point for us, and everyone had left without me. I was really anxious about how I would reach, and then I saw Ganesh—he was the only one waiting for me at the platform. He had arrived at seven-thirty in the morning and had waited till about one-thirty in the afternoon, which is when I reached. I was so happy to see him, I remember I let go of the bar I was holding for support in the train while it was still moving and fell down on to the platform! He came running to help me, and I hugged him tight and kissed him all over the face. He still remembers how I left lipstick marks everywhere!

Eventually Ganesh came into the hijra community as well and became Gauri—she went in for gender-confirmation surgery as well.

Gauri's own family disowned her. She'd lost her mother at a young age, and her father simply asked her to leave home one day because he couldn't take the cross-dressing and the taunts of his social and professional circles any more. Gauri was working at the Humsafar Trust then and she moved out and started living on her own. Her life has been one of monumental struggle. It's not easy going through all that, and the surgery—the medication, the counselling—all alone. My biological family took Gauri under its wing and became like a family to her, she says. She can come home and ask my mother to cook for her, take a nap in my bedroom . . . we can exert these rights on each other. So much so that she even walks off with my saris at times! I'll see her wearing it one fine day and then she'll say, 'If I had asked you, you wouldn't have given it to me because you're so possessive about your sari collection. So I just decided to take it with me.'

I can also pour my heart out to her—I have even cried on her shoulder in my weaker moments. No matter what, I know she's there for me whenever I need her.

It's been twenty years and counting since we first met, and Gauri remembers me the way I was all those years ago. She likes to talk about my first TV appearance way back in 1998. It was a role in a serial called *Ghungroo* that was on hijras. Gauri recalls the exact moment on the show when I, dressed in a gorgeous yellow sari and red bangles, twirl my long plait with my wrist and say, '*Amma jhooth na bulwaye* (Don't make me lie, mother).' For years, she would repeat that line to me and tease me, saying, '*Laxmi, jhooth na bulwaye.*'

Gauri has come such a long way. Today she's the director of Sakhi Char Chowghi, a community-based (hijra- and TG-based) HIV/AIDS organization. Gauri and I have worked together on many issues, travelled together to international conferences, to Australia and the US. (I helped her with her paperwork and related things.) I have also helped her draft presentations several times. She tells me that my nudging her has played a big role in her achievements, and that makes me feel very special.

Gauri also looks out for me—especially since I have gained fame and become a known face. Sometimes, she'll pity me for it! Like this one time when we went to Ajmer Sharif together—Gauri had never visited and I was going, so I asked her to come along. This was soon after I came out of the *Bigg Boss* house, so a lot of people at the dargah spotted me and soon there was a mob around us. It was very difficult for us to leave the dargah, and it took us almost five hours to walk that barely ten-minute distance! Gauri said to me, 'I'm glad I can eat pani puri anywhere, but you can't!' Another time I remember we were in the car together, going from Thane to Vashi, when a hijra at the traffic light saw us and started asking me to get off and talk to her. At that same moment, the light turned green and we sped off. But I asked the driver to turn the car around and go back there. Both Gauri and I got out of the car, sat down with that hijra and had cutting chai. Soon enough, a crowd had gathered there, but the happiness of that hijra made it all worthwhile.

Meena Saraswathi Seshu and Anjali Gopalan are two of my very close friends and I include them in my book about men not only because they are symbols of strength for me, but also because of the running joke between us that Meena and Anjali are my husbands from past lives, reborn as women in this one! Both Meena and Anjali are very possessive about me; they always say they'll bash up any man who tries to disturb my peace of mind. And they look like sisters, too—my strong feminist friends. We met in 2006 when we were all in Toronto for work, and were hanging out together—Meena, Anjali and I. Both of them kept telling me to behave myself, behave like this and like that—'*itni masti mat kar*', they kept saying. I was in my man-hating phase at the time, so I told them both, 'Please. I'll only listen to what my husband says. You're not my husbands that I should listen to you.' Right then and there they both decided and said that they are! So, that's how that joke began. Meena and Anjali make better men than most men because they are such strong women.

Meena, a social activist from the Tata Institute of Social Sciences, is the secretary-general of Sampada Gramin Mahila Sanstha (SANGRAM, an HIV/AIDS prevention, treatment and support organization working with socially marginalized people in Sangli, Maharashtra) and works primarily with sex workers. She has such an inspiring presence. She has dedicated her life completely and entirely to bettering the lives of sex workers, and has given her all to the community. Besides Andrew Hunter, it was Meena who was responsible for my being drawn into sex-work activism.

I remember when we were flying to Toronto for a conference, we had a hilarious episode! There was this scare of liquid bombs that was in the news then. At the time, I didn't have breasts, so I would put water balloons in my bra. I had already decided that if airport security objected, I'd remove them and throw them in the dustbin, but I'd take the chance anyway. I cleared the security check, nobody caught anything. I stepped away from the security check and walked over to where Meena and the others were sitting. Meena was telling them how her medicines had been confiscated. She's diabetic and has to carry insulin with her. She had kept a very tiny amount of it in her bag, just as a precautionary measure for the flight, but the security personnel had taken it away without even listening to her. Naturally, the poor thing was upset about it and also anxious about the journey. And here I was with water in my bra! So I told her, 'What liquid are you talking about? I have water balloons on my body and nobody said anything to me.' She just looked at me and almost instantly, her anxiety turned into amusement—she burst out laughing. She wasn't disgruntled for the rest of the journey, and for that entire trip that joke never became stale. I kept tripping on it with Meena. 'Oh, but nobody stopped me for the water balloons in my bra!' I'd say, and she'd reply, 'My meds were taken away from me, but not Laxmi's fake water breasts!' And each time we'd be in fits!

Meena's work is in Sangli and she works with many trans people and I can see that has really influenced her deeply, because of how utterly sensitized she is to our needs and our pain. She always says that she's learnt a lot from me and from those she works with in Sangli. I feel I have picked up so much from her as an activist, but she'll always insist that I have educated her. In New York, where we were together for a conference, I remember turning around to her and asking, 'Meena, am I invisible?' And she said, 'No, sweetheart, you are definitely not.' 'Why is there no acknowledgement of us as human beings then?' I pressed. Meena was struck by that. She believes my activism is pure because it has not evolved from positions of academic interest or nuances of legalese. That I have that basic ground-level instinctive knowledge and awareness that comes from the lived experience of having been marginalized myself for a large part of my life. And that's why my understanding and reactions and how I am as an activist are all linked to that and intertwined. That's such an astute view, and of course, she's absolutely right. Over the years I have matured as an activist, and today I am polished, no longer the naive, awestruck person who'd gone to the UN in New York back in 2008. In those days I was just someone trying to grapple with the issues of the community and understand them. So I was asking a question like that—we are a visible community, so why no policies? My understanding of activism was, in a way, shaped during that conference in New York—again something that Meena has articulated for me. Trying to comprehend what happens within certain communities and why these communities need advocacy became very clear to me. Trans people in sex work, males and females in sex work, the MSM and trans issues, drug users—all had gathered together to speak about their varied rights as distinct communities. But the way I saw it was that whoever the state criminalizes for whatever reason actually come under one umbrella. I think that gave me that broader understanding of activism. Meena insists that that's what gives me the ability to reach out to a large group of people. It's because I don't get entrenched in any one political ideology. I'd rather talk about people and human rights. Older activists like herself, she says, find it very tough to bridge these so easily because of their personal political ideologies.

We often discuss our personal lives also, covering a wide range of topics. I'll talk to her at length about the kinnar *akhara*, my pet project realized with the precious support of spiritual guru Rishi Ajaydas and Kamla bua (the first transgender to be elected mayor in 1999, from Katni in Madhya Pradesh), which saw its successful launch at the Ujjain Kumbh in April 2016. And I know that even though Meena has no real understanding of what I'm saying, she'll hear me out and offer good advice. I also know that she's a complete atheist, but still I'll keep going on and on about the power of religion and converting people to activism through religion and she'll discuss with me at length the social and political implications of all that. She listens no matter what I have to say and that's how our relationship has developed. If I talk about my boyfriends and the ups and downs of my love life, she'll tell me, 'Laxmi, with you it's all such extreme ups and downs. When the up is up, it's all super-fantastic, everything is beyond amazing. But when the down is down, it's all terrible, it's very low.' But what can I do? That's just my personality—I've always been like that in a way, in my personal life—swinging between extremes. Meena is right; that's why I get disappointed so very fast and elated equally fast. So whether I'm regaling her with my elation, or depressing with my disappointment, she'll tell me to shut up either way! Meena has also pointed it out as a huge weakness of mine. 'Be very careful about it, because it can really be a deterrent to your health,' she says to me often, and quite lovingly. She'll try and boost my morale when I need it, or just hold my hand or put things in perspective and help me maintain my balance, I feel. I'll just be ranting about something to her and she'll just say, 'Okay, Laxmi. Now take a deep breath.' It has a calming effect on me instantly. Meena is very protective of me. She feels that I make a lot of enemies and that I do need some manner of protection. Of course I'm very protective too—I feel I can go to any lengths to protect the people I love, like her. We don't meet too often because she lives in Sangli and each time she is in Mumbai, she's at the airport, mostly to travel outside the state or the country.

Meena is so very strong in her own right—with tremendous drama, I declared that she is my *prananaath*, a term that tickles her no end. Of course we've been having fun with it, but Meena also has such a fine understanding of human nature and gender that she has a deeper take on the topic. She tells me that my declaring that, in a way, presents the construct of how maybe we're all ultimately trans. In many aspects, Meena is very strong, characterized by typical male qualities, and so, the way I see it, she is definitely different from the very feminine version of femininity that is practised and privileged, and then there is a need to characterize one as the other. Meena's argument is that perhaps in some kind of continuum, women like her occupy more of an 'other' space than the typical feminine space. By naming her my husband, I am recognizing those characteristics in her and painting her with those brushstrokes. We all have both in us, after all, and we choose to only express one or the other at any given point in time.

Anjali is a force of nature. We can say that she single-handedly brought up the issue of Section 377. She is such a hard-working lady; her commitment to her causes, whether it is human rights or animal rights, is amazing! She is absolutely an inspirational figure for me. We met in 2002 during the press conference in Mumbai—Vikram Doctor was there too—where the conch was blown for Section 377 after Anjali had filed the case. But we really got to know each other at the Toronto conference when we travelled together and spent some time with each other.

Anjali has always appreciated me for what she calls my courage, which enables me to speak my mind at all costs. She looks at me as someone sincerely prepared to put herself on the line and be out there, no matter what. That's what drew her to me. 'Here's an individual

I need to get to know because of the person she is. She is absolutely straightforward about what she has to say, and says things openly without beating around the bush,' she has said about me. She also worries about me for the same reason, especially given the current political environment in the country that, according to her, seems to be a time when we simply don't know what might happen to anyone.

Over the years we have grown to love each other, and our relationship has really evolved and strengthened. I earnestly feel that relationships such as the one I have with Anjali are what're going to keep our heads above water when the time comes. There's also a very deep respect between us. It's like what Anjali says about new families these days, how we're living in an age where we're defining family very differently. That family doesn't necessarily mean the ties we are born into; it is also the very powerful bonds that we forge as we grow older. Anjali tells me that when she takes a pause in life and wonders about who all are her family, she invariably thinks of a few remarkable individuals who are a part of her life—people she feels blessed to have in her life. I am so honoured and happy to be one of those individuals, to be part of this redefined family—and to know at the back of my mind that I don't have to worry, they'll be there for me. We don't even have to speak to each other or stay in touch out of formality or anything—we do it because we want to, there're no social impositions. Sometimes I wonder how these relationships happen in life, but thank god they do! We would all be so much poorer emotionally if they didn't materialize the way they did.

Anjali tells me that I'm a WYSIWYG sort of person—there are no ruses, there's nothing hidden with me, whatever I have to say, whoever I am, is all upfront. And while she appreciates this quality in me, she also thinks it is a point of concern. 'There are too few people in our country who are able to speak their minds any more. Your ability to do that and not care about how the world is viewing you is remarkable and at the same time, something you need to learn to protect yourself from, especially in the current political climate,' she says.

My persistence keeps her going too, she says, which is really humbling, because to me, Anjali is a shining source of inspiration. But I think for many people like us who are doing the kind of work we're doing, we draw strength from each other. When you're in doubt, people like Anjali make the path you're on so very clear again. It's like we're all shining beacons on each other's life paths. It helps you stay on the path when you're feeling hopeless—we need that from each other. She respects me tremendously as an activist just as I do her and Meena. Anjali always says that in this kind of work, you can never separate the personal and the political. It's your personal truth that you're fighting for. That's why I feel we've all been instrumental in putting a law into place for a community.

Anjali also calls me 'a beautiful woman with unbelievable confidence', which sends me over the moon, of course, and that's why I say she's my husband. She always laughs and says, 'How could any man resist you, Laxmi?' When I call her up because I'm feeling low, she's always there to listen to me. Even if she doesn't agree with the relationship choices I have made—and I know she doesn't—she'll give me gyan often enough. But whoever listens when you're in love? Definitely not me! Still, she'll tell me, 'I worry about you. Someone like you should not be made use of by men who are unscrupulous.' But I know if something goes wrong and I fall hard, she'll be there for me. She warns me about it, because when you fall in love with someone, you forget what's important, and you may change your strong personality, make adjustments. And then it becomes impossible to turn back.

I once told her, 'You think like a man. And you're the kind of husband I've always wanted. So you're my husband number one.' She promptly responded, 'You better not forget that!' Occasionally, when I'm feeling beat and depressed, she'll try to cheer me up and say with a chuckle, 'You know what you need, Laxmi? You need more husbands like me!'

With Meena and Anjali, distance and time do not matter. A year can pass by without so much as a hello—but when we meet or talk, our time apart just melts away. We just pick up the threads of our conversation from wherever we were the last time we spoke.

I met Varsha Gaikwad when she was the minister for women and child development in Maharashtra. She had come from the Women's Mission meeting at the Sahyadri Guest House. Everyone there was discussing only women sex workers and so I got up and said, 'Where are we? My community is also into sex work, what about our rights? No political party has ever taken it up as a cause or commitment. What about the third gender?' Despite all the nay-saying around her, Varsha said that the government must take responsibility for transgenders as well, and I've had immense respect for her ever since. We formed expert subcommittees at that meeting, comprising scholars and social workers, whose sole purpose would be to look into issues concerning hijras. We discussed sensitization workshops at the school level, to treat third-gender children as children with special needs, because really, that's the kind of intervention we need at that stage to ensure transgenders are not opting out of mainstream systems, or being pushed out, due to the serious discrimination they face. We spoke about the need for proper documentation for adults—how they needed access to ration cards, Aadhaar cards, passports. When the third women's policy was being drafted, Varsha called me and asked if I would take on the responsibility because I had spoken about inclusion, and mentioned that we should have our own chapter in the policy. I immediately agreed and she made me the coordinator for the chapter, so that both women and transgenders could be embraced within the policy. She went on to become the force that was protecting the right of transgenders in the Maharashtra welfare board. If we got the policy approved by the Cabinet, we only have her remarkable commitment to thank, because she was the one who presented our recommendations to the chief minister.

Varsha goes to her constituency every evening, works very hard. I admire and respect her. She comes from a Dalit family and has really proved herself in an arena dominated by men.

Dorothea Riecker is a German journalist who's a very serious Indophile and has been living in India for decades now, having made Delhi her home. I met her during the making of the *Between the Lines* documentary—she was part of the team and doing the research for it. Someone had set up a meeting with Lata guru for Dorothea and I remember walking into that meeting, noticing that poor Dorothea was being grilled for no reason by Lata guru! She was absolutely cornered and to this day, when she tells the story, she says, 'Laxmi actually rescued me from that meeting!' We went on to work together on the film, and became very good friends. She's one of my oldest friends in Delhi, I've known her for over fifteen years. Dorothea has stayed with me in my home in Mumbai— she knows my sisters, my entire family. She is very keen on understanding the issues of the community and I can safely say that she appreciates them very well now; she's totally immersed in them.

I've been fortunate to have met and worked with some amazing queer-identifying professionals in my activism, people who have since become my friends. Ernest Noronha, who left the Humsafar Trust and is today project manager at UNDP India, and Joe Wong, a trans man from Singapore who is programme manager at the Asia Pacific Transgender Network that I co-founded, are two such people. Ernest is also chela to Gauri, and because she lost her mother to cancer, we became close. I feel I'm like a mother to her. I met Joe when the second APTN meeting happened in Bangkok, and I am very supportive of all his initiatives there.

I met Raju Iyer for work reasons. Raju is in infrastructure; he's into power-brokering and negotiating and the go-to man in Thane to get jobs done. Through him I met and became very close to his wife, Naina Iyer, and indeed the entire family. Raju and I have a love–hate relationship, in that we love to hate each other! Whenever we meet, it's a huge clash of personalities—he's alpha male and, of course, I'm alpha female, so it's an absolute storm! We keep hurtling abuses at each other—it's even how we greet each other—and poor Naina always has to shut her ears beyond a point! Of course, it's all in jest and the spirit of friendship.

I remember going to their place in Thane with Raju at some godforsaken hour and that's when Naina and I first met. We were ravenous because we'd had a very busy day and hadn't really eaten much, and that lady cooked rajma–chawal for us at 4 a.m.! I'll never forget the taste of that meal—it was delicious, of course, but more than anything else, the fact that she made it for us then, added to its taste. Raju and I have our ups and downs—there have been times when neither has spoken to the other for months—but my relationship with Naina has always been rock-steady. In fact, she turns negotiator when Raju and I are going through a rough patch and is relieved when it's over—of course we might be arguing on the outside, but both of us keep pestering Naina for news about the other person! Raju always tells Naina that the one thing he has learnt from me is how to ignore someone completely, make it such that that person doesn't even exist.

Naina is one of the very few people whom I can call myself with updates and information about the new things happening in my life—if there is an achievement I am proud of, or an international conference I've been invited to, I make sure to call her, because I really feel she's my well-wisher. I often call her on my way to the airport to tell her where I'm jet-setting off to next, and she's one of the very first people I call when I'm back in India. I can go to their place any time—Naina tells me there'll always be a room ready for me—and cry my heart out if I'm feeling low. She also discusses her problems with me. A while ago, she wanted to help someone who was HIV positive and I did everything I could to help her with that situation. When Naina was looking for a private tutor for her kids, I recommended Praveen's name and he started going there for tuitions. Often, we've all met after the tuitions, and talked and laughed late into the evening. We have such a strong bond now that when people gossip about Raju and me and our 'relationship'—which is an Indian obsession—it doesn't bother her in the least. 'I know my husband,' she says, and adds, 'and most importantly, I know Laxmi.' She's so very open and free with me—I have a terrible habit of forgetting birthdays, it's just one of those things where my memory fails me. So Naina will call me up on her birthday and say, 'Laxmi, please wish me.'

I never step out in public without my make-up— everyone knows this about me. I think Raju and Naina's house is the only place where I've gone without any make-up. I just ring the doorbell as I am, Naina will open the door, and I'm absolutely comfortable walking in and talking about anything and everything. I also adore their boys—now they're all grown-up, one is sixteen and the other's twenty-two, but I remember when they were younger and looking for some career counselling, I was summoned to their house to discuss options. At the end of the discussion, I looked at her and said, '*Hai na, Naina?*' and she replied, 'Yes, Laxmi. Of course. You're right.'

Radhe Maa is part of my book for the sheer courage she has. Especially after all the controversies she has faced, which have all been rubbish, if you ask me.

I've known her for a long, long time, before any of this media attention started. I'm very close to her, I've always loved her, and she thinks of me as a daughter. She's a very simple soul, a beautiful soul, yet so much negativity has been piled on her by the world. I know that people will say I feel this way because I am a devotee, but no, it's because I've known her for a long time and because I *know* she is a genuine person—I respect her immensely. She's a very spiritual person, and emanates only positive energy. I perceive and sense people as energies, somehow I have always done that, and that's how I know.

Becoming a goddess figure and going under the media lens—this whole trial by media—is such trauma. But she has the courage to stand there strong. When a woman enters this world of spirituality, everything comes under attack—and her character in particular is assassinated immediately. The same has happened to Radhe Maa—because godmen are fine, nobody questions them, but what about godwomen?

I've known about spiritual guru Rishi Ajaydas ever since I came back from the *Bigg Boss* house—he'd written a book on hijras, titled *Tratiya Prakriti Kinnar*, and has been proactive about our cause of emancipating hijras in India. We finally met when he asked me to come to Ujjain—Viki had to go anyway to give his exams for the Central Industrial Security Force, so we went together. And I found the rishi to be a *suljha hua aadmi ekdum* (a sorted man), and a very genuine human being. The idea for the kinnar akhara had its proper birth then. He has an important presence in Ujjain, and was extremely helpful during the entire process, right from procuring the land, to the execution of the events. This was a historic moment for us—for the first time ever, kinnars had an exclusive space at the Ujjain Kumbh Mela in 2016—and he was greatly responsible for making it happen. We decided on the first day of the Navratras in October 2015, a holy day, and we established the akhara as well. We called hijras from fourteen states, from our networks, and decided to have ten *peetha*s in ten directions and assign *peethadakshya*s to each.

The akhara was an absolute success; we made news everywhere! So many hijras from across the length and breadth of the country came there and also took the *shahi snan* (ritualistic bath) at the Kumbh. The energy was electric! I was given the distinct honour of being made the Acharya Mahamandaleshwara of the kinnar akhara—the highest rank—there. The rishi has now become a great friend of mine—such a deeply spiritual and humble soul.

You make some connections in life that aren't so easy to explain. Viki Patil, the owner of Rukhmini Dhaba, popularly known as the Mankoli Dhaba, located on the Mumbai–Nashik highway, is one such. I used to frequent his dhaba a lot and we had a cordial relationship—the food was great, and to him, I was a celebrity visitor whose pictures he would put up in his dhaba. When a son was born to him, he invited me for the naming ceremony, but on the day it totally slipped my mind. But then he called me and said he would wait for me to arrive, so I remember I dropped what I was doing and went to the function he had organized all the way from Sion! Since then, we've had a deep friendship—he calls me Mamma and he calls Viki (Thomas) Papa, which is funny because he's so much older than Viki.

Some people you meet seem like mirror images of yourself—it's like looking into a river of reflection, which shows you an old self come back to meet you. One of Atharv's and my friend, Krish Thapa, whom we lovingly refer to as Jateshwari Kris because of his dreadlocks and braids, is one such person. I'm not sure I understand his sexuality, but he acts like a woman and is absolute crazy fun to be with. Krish reminds me of myself when I was that age, in my early twenties, so young and carefree. I am calmer now and quite the serious worker, but I used to be the untamed Laxmi once—the one who never gave a damn, who thought the world could burn and rot, whom nobody or nothing could intimidate—which is an exact description of Jateshwari Kris. It's a blast just being around energy like that and it's surreal for me. I think that's where my love for her comes from because I'm not like that any more—I have a persona that I do try and consciously maintain—but it's fun and in a way important for me to see that and reminding myself from time to time who I was. Just soaking in that energy of my past shadow that has come back to me—it preserves me and my self today, in a way.

PRINCE MANVENDRA'S MONOLOGUE: LAXMI, MY SISTER

·◈· Prince Manvendra Singh Gohil of Rajpipla
in Gujarat is the first openly gay member
of India's royalty. ·◈·

When I was a little child, I was scared of hijras. When I refused to eat my food or was fussy about finishing something on my plate, my nani would admonish me, saying in a threatening tone, 'Eat it, or I'll call the hijras . . . Finish this, or a hijra will come get you.'

Nanima should see me now—I have a sister who is hijra, whom I am incredibly, extremely close to. I first met Laxmi in the late 1990s. Maybe in 1996 or '97. Perhaps at the Humsafar offices, a trust that Ashok Row Kavi—Laxmi's godfather who introduced me into the gay world and helped me in those early days—started in 1995, around the same time that I got in touch with him.

Laxmi was very young then—in her teens and I still have an image of her in my head, of a young boy in a shirt and trousers. Back then, Laxmi wasn't hijra. When I close my eyes and think in retrospect, I see a sweet little boy clinging to a doll in his arms. Even though she was so young and I was already a man. Thirty-two—so much older than her—a man with childlike simplicity, and amazingly feminine. Even today, the way she speaks and thinks—she is much more mature than I am. I often feel that I'm behaving like a child in front of her. My upbringing was completely different to hers or anyone else's for that matter. I was not exposed to much of the world, let alone the gay world. I was struggling at that point, trying to come to terms with my own sexuality, completely baffled by my feelings. I did not have courage then. It was only in 2002 that I was able to muster the strength to come out to my family, and then to the world in 2006. Ashok mentored me in a way, and on one of those Fridays—that's when Humsafar would hold their meetings—I met the phenomenon called Laxmi. She personified courage then, and ever since. I truly believe she was already a phenomenon then. I found in her a very high level of confidence and of course great ambition—she has always been very ambitious about what she wanted to achieve.

A considerably long span of time passed before our paths crossed again and when they did and we met again, Laxmi was already a hijra, inducted into the community. She was infused with even more self-confidence and certainty to exert and assert her own identity. By then I had started my own organization, the Lakshya Trust (which I still run), and had just begun working in Surat, which has the largest hijra population in Gujarat, 600 hijras, and is also one of the oldest gharanas. In 2001 we got a government project to work specifically with transgenders and hijras, which was a big milestone for us. But no sooner had we taken it on than we began facing huge difficulties getting through to the gharanas and hijras. They simply refused to communicate with us. It seemed our pilot project was doomed!

Laxmi had made quite a name for herself when I got in touch with her again and formally invited her to Surat as the chief guest at a dance contest we were organizing in 2003. I was hoping it would help us make inroads within the hijra community and it worked beautifully. The fact that she accepted our invitation and came down to Surat with two of her chelas—that someone of her stature had agreed to grace the occasion—turned out to be the deal-maker for Lakshya and us. Not only did she come all the way to attend the event, she also gave a dance performance herself. That did not go unnoticed; it was because of her visit that our intervention process with the hijras gained headway and began shaping up well. When she came to Surat, she openly told the gurus that Lakshya was doing a wonderful job and that they ought to cooperate with us. What we'd been trying for so long and frankly struggling with, Laxmi accomplished in under two minutes flat. After that, there was no looking back. Once the gurus were convinced, the chelas followed. What the guru says, the chela will always do—only if the guru tells the chela to wear a condom will he ever do that! We managed to do tremendous work, and our project is now counted as a success story. And I happily give Laxmi all the credit for starting us off. Since then, we've done so much work, built a lot of goodwill and trust in the community—so much so that even our staff is hijra now. We started with the issues of HIV and AIDS prevention and control, and today, we've expanded our scope of work. We now do extensive work on social security issues as well as rehabilitation. Laxmi has always been supportive of us and our work. In some ways, it also helped that we were working in different states—there was no sense of competition between us and our organizations and the work we were doing. Also, in Gujarat, I think I can safely say we were the only ones, so we were away from the Mumbai political scene—it can get quite bizarre and ugly there.

Laxmi is a natural leader—all her amazing qualities contribute to her personality as a leader. Seeing her in such a position of power also helps combat the social stigma around hijras. I remember when my guruji, from whom I learnt music, met Laxmi at one of my birthday dos.

He must have been around eighty-five then—he died at ninety-one—and had nursed a bad opinion of hijras all his life. But the moment I introduced Laxmi, I could see his entire impression of hijras change. In a matter of a few hours, they were both chatting like old buddies, and it was obvious that he had shed all his preconceived notions about hijras. And this has happened time and again—I have been witness to it. Another myth that's perpetually circulated about hijras is that they are wicked and nasty towards children, that they kidnap them and castrate the boys and all that. But Laxmi is wonderful with kids. I have seen parents handing over their kids to her themselves—imagine a parent doing that! It's because she is extremely loving towards children. When you see it with your own eyes is when you realize how unfounded the fear is and how it needs to be wiped away from our minds. There has been a change in the impression of hijras that people have had all their lives—I would say that Laxmi has made that happen single-handedly. Even I can be called an example of that! Once we were both having dinner in Thane at a restaurant and there was a child who had come there to dine with his parents and was constantly crying. Laxmi gave him such a loving smile from our table that the child stopped crying almost instantly. I remember even the mother was grateful.

One singularly great talent of hers, which has held her in good stead because of how useful it is, is her absolute command over public speaking. Her oratory skills are tremendous and one of the many things that I've been trying to learn from her. My speeches, I feel, tend to get philosophical and perhaps too theoretical, which can leave the audience distracted. But she can captivate any kind of audience and speak for hours together without any of the listeners feeling bored. I've seen all kinds of audiences honouring her with standing ovations. When she was touring Gujarat for the launch of the Gujarati translation of her first book *Me Hijra, Me Laxmi*, I was accompanying her. She gave such a motivational speech at MSU University, Vadodara, that the dean and students stood up at the end and applauded for a long time. So Laxmi got a resounding ovation there. At another event, as I recall, Laxmi spoke about how hijras could be employed as security guards— because they'll never touch women—and how it would lend dignity of life to the community. This is a point she repeats often; she has even said this on national radio, in fact, and it's such a valid point to have transgender police guards. Others could say it too, and they might even have, but it was really brought home when Laxmi talked about it because of the way she speaks, her public speaking skills. At a university she was speaking to the students about Section 377 and she started by talking about masturbation. 'Is there anyone in this hall, in the audience, who doesn't masturbate?' she asked, her voice booming across the auditorium. She spoke of sex as a basic need and then she listed the primary facts of the case. The way she presents the argument, I feel as if you immediately know there's something to think about. Her connect is instant and electric! She's also very well versed in the Vedas and other Hindu texts—it's because she belongs to a well-respected Brahmin family and grew up learning about them—and is thus able to instil and imbue meaning in each and every word she speaks. She'll go into mythology, history, religion, armed with tremendous insight, and make her case. Again, that's the beauty of Laxmi's public persona—so many people are as knowledgeable as her, if not more, but they are not able to put it across as well and so are unable to communicate with an audience. To retain the knowledge and talk about it in public, you must know how to present it—it's no easy task but she has the knack for it.

Laxmi also knows how to build relationships and then maintain them, making sure they remain intact. She's the kind of person who wouldn't want to break off with anyone who has come into her life unless the relationship itself has seriously deteriorated and turned into something that she cannot handle, or if the person has really harmed her. Then of course Laxmi can bite and how! She can be very nasty when she is in her full-on hijrotic mode! Otherwise she's the kind of person who would rather work on a relationship than break it off entirely—I quite admire this about her.

Which is why I was very shocked to find out suddenly that Lata guru, her hijra guru with whom she had a very close relationship, was no longer part of Laxmi's life. It was almost as if Lata guru or Lata rani as she was often called, had disappeared! Lata rani was close to me too, but only because of Laxmi. I was once given the most unpleasant responsibility of flying with Lata rani from Mumbai to Delhi. Oh, I had a harrowing time! She created such a tamasha! First with the security check and the rule about liquids. Then, she's addicted to paan and she's constantly chewing it. So when we were on board and she wanted to spit it out, she thought she could just do it in the aisle! Thankfully I stopped her just in the nick of time. She's such a loud person that everyone around was disturbed by her and of course they were all staring at me. She started grumbling about buying snacks on the plane—'How can you take money from hijras? Hijras are supposed to take money from you!'

she was screaming at them. She didn't let me pay either and then she started clapping, threatening them for free biscuits! And then as if all this wasn't enough, she bad-mouthed Laxmi throughout the flight, complaining to me about her non-stop. How she wears indecent clothes and short skirts and cleavage-revealing tops and how that's not appropriate. '*Yeh hamaare gharane ki naak katwa rahi hai* (She is tarnishing the reputation of our gharana),' she wailed. '*Aap uske bhai saab hain—usko samjhao* (You are her elder brother, you must make her understand).' And then, at the meeting in Delhi that we were attending, she fell asleep! She was snoring! I refused to accompany her on the way back. I said that I'd rather go by bullock cart if I had to, but not with her! Laxmi was quite faithful to Lata rani from what I had seen, but then suddenly one day she was not with Lata guru and not part of the DWS either. It was a little surprising for me, because there had been genuine affection between them. Lata rani was proud of Laxmi in many ways too, and Laxmi was always very loyal to her and tried to meet her dictates. That's the only time I was surprised by Laxmi—the fact that this relationship ended was most uncharacteristic of her. But there must have been strong reasons for Laxmi to take that decision; it's not like her to take such a step without justification.

Even the parties she throws, mostly to celebrate her birthday, are proof of that. It's like a full-fledged event, an absolute blast! The entire LGBT community is there, of course, in full show. As is her biological family—her mother, her father when he was alive, her brother who usually acts as emcee, her sister and brother-in-law, her nephews. The police are there as are known goons—I've never been to a party where the police and the goons are socializing with each other! There are politicians from almost every party, be it BJP, Congress, CPI(M), you name it. You'll find Bollywood celebrities there too, and the media. I always cite it as an example to people: If you ever want to see mainstreaming, go to Laxmi's birthday parties, I say. It's a shining example of what can be achieved, what is possible. She hasn't thrown a party in a while though, I really miss them.

There's so much to learn from Laxmi as a leader. Each time I meet her, I feel I have learnt something new. She calls herself a learning process, an unfinished project, which is why she always has that energy about her. Another thing she's doing brilliantly as a leader is that she's preparing the next generation. Laxmi knows that there has to be the next Laxmi, a new Laxmi, a younger Laxmi, who can continue her fight and believe in the cause, and so she's really preparing some of her chelas to that end. I can see that she's trying to train and empower them to be the second in line, somebody who can take charge and be in command. I don't know if it is possible to create another Laxmi; there can be only one *Laxmi*. But Laxmi is trying, like a good leader must.

A magnanimous heart and true generosity of spirit define Laxmi. She was called by a university in Pune that gives out national awards in different fields and they were starting a new category for excellence in the field of social service. It was momentous that they were giving the award to a trans person and as part of their process, they asked Laxmi to recommend a name for the following year's award. She immediately nominated mine, and so I was given the award on 7 February 2016. So far no sexual minority group has been given this honour and it's a matter of great prestige. It's just like Laxmi to nominate someone who she thinks is doing good work. Most activists, you'll find, are selfish in nature. But not Laxmi, she's very generous. And this is something she keeps doing on a regular basis. She's referred me to so many people, I keep getting calls from people directed to me by her. She's brought me on to several TV shows and interviews also, like *Raaz Pichle Janam Ka*. In fact she also recommended me for *Bigg*

Boss after she participated in the show, but I refused to go on that!

She's emphatic in her ways, which makes Laxmi a force of nature. I remember being part of a conference with her in 2005 in Vadodara. We were all gathered in a conference room at the Express Alkapuri hotel and the air conditioner was not working. We were all very uncomfortable, naturally, but Laxmi was perhaps the most uneasy because of her make-up. So she went straight to the manager's office. We were told he was in a board meeting, but Laxmi demanded to meet with him and just stormed in. She asked him directly, in the middle of his meeting, for the air conditioner to be fixed. He explained that there was some problem with it, and that it would take some time, but she was adamant. She said, 'I don't know anything, you fix this AC now, otherwise I'm going to become a typical hijra and lift my sari and petticoat.' The manager panicked. I don't think he'd ever seen or met anyone like her. Needless to say, the air conditioner was repaired in no time, in the next few moments, in fact! After that, during the course of our stay there, the entire hotel staff was like *'Laxmi ji ko chai mili ki nahi* (Did Laxmi ji get tea)?' *'Laxmi ji ka naashta laao* (Bring Laxmi ji's snack).' Even when we were checking out and clearing the payment, they were all telling us, *'Arre, kya jaldi hai payment ki? Koi jaldi nahi hai* (There is no rush to clear the payment).' She has these tactics of getting things done—it's an art; she knows how to work the situation to her best advantage.

She's a genius at getting payments that have been pending forever. She even helped Ashok with it, as I recall. His biological mother's pension money was stuck and he had been trying forever to claim it, he'd even asked the police but of course nothing had happened. He requested Laxmi and she got it collected in some twenty-four hours! And she didn't even go herself, she sent someone who paid up at the mention of her name. It wasn't even a small amount, I believe, it was close to Rs 8 lakh!

Laxmi has her faults of course, like all of us. Nobody's perfect, right? I would say that Laxmi trusts people too fast and too easily. She's not necessarily a great judge of character and that becomes a fault. She puts blind faith in a person and there have been times when she's regretted it, but by then it's too late. And when you're of the stature of Laxmi, this becomes a huge negative. I would say that about her current boyfriend Viki Thomas as well. She herself has asked me about Viki lots of times and I have told her quite bluntly that I don't think he's someone she should invest so much time in. I've told her not to give him too much importance in her life. I'm quite straightforward that way and we have that kind of an equation. I also feel that she has reached a certain stage in life where she needs to be extremely choosy about whom to trust and whom not to. Because betrayal is something that she might not be able to afford at this stage, it might be too expensive for her.

We were in Gandhinagar together some time ago. Usually Viki is always around and we can't talk too openly, but this time she was travelling without him, so we were speaking freely. My husband Duke was with me and we were all hanging out together at night and, as it happens, we started talking about intimate matters. Duke is a card reader—he's a very spiritually inclined person, and likes to meditate. He doesn't read cards as a profession, but these thoughts come to him naturally. His readings are also quite accurate. So he said the same thing to her about Viki. Duke warned her that she should not trust people too easily and he specifically said that about Viki whom he has also met. We both told her that she's getting too emotionally involved with him and that he might take undue advantage of her and her reputation. 'You'll have an emotional breakdown,' I tried to make her understand, 'so it's better to take precautions in the beginning of the relationship.' She was quite disappointed; that someone you love deeply could betray you is not something you want to hear, ever. Her face changed completely when Duke did those readings.

Laxmi often seeks my advice on personal matters like this and in other spheres of her life because I think she knows that I have no selfish interest in influencing her one way or another. And so my advice will be completely free of bias. That's another reason why she has close ties with me, because she knows I have no personal agenda or interest in giving her advice. Many other people around her might have a vested interest in either her NGO or even in her personal life, but not me.

At times Laxmi's behaviour is questionable too. She'll nurse ego issues or throw around attitude. I understand that some of it comes with fame and popularity and I don't think there's anything wrong with it per se, but it could be damaging because it might hamper her relations with people. Of course, she doesn't throw her weight around with me. I'm a born celebrity, and having lived with public attention all my life, I know how to handle it. But her I-am-something behaviour can be detrimental at times. We always say that too much ego is not a good thing and it's something she needs to be mindful of as she becomes more popular and gains more respect. I have heard too many stories of how she keeps people waiting, how she has no respect for time and takes another's time for granted—at least half a dozen people have told me this about her. I think I will advise her on this soon—when I see it happening in front of me, I will definitely tell her to keep it in check.

Anyone who thinks Laxmi is being difficult to manage, usually comes to me, saying, 'You're the only one who can handle Laxmi, please help us.' When we travel together for conferences, the organizers often tell me that she is my responsibility, and so I should be sure that she wakes up early enough and is on time for the event. Now I know that her make-up itself is a process that takes an hour or two, so I have to bear that in mind. Sometimes I get quite anxious about it. Once, when we were in Delhi, she threw a tantrum about the size of the hotel room she'd been put up in by the event organizers. Apparently the hotel people had been told by the organizers to contact me if there was any problem with Laxmi because I would be able to handle it. Luckily, I was also staying at the same hotel then, and I eventually managed to pacify her. I offered to switch rooms with her, and that mollified her to some extent. People find her difficult at times, but I think she's the sweetest. Maybe I feel that way because she listens to me! I know that she loves me as only a sister can. When she talks about me, she always says things like 'I'm so proud of my brother, he's a prince and he has no airs, he's a very down-to-earth person.' She's very proud to have a brother like me—that I know.

Our relationship is very special. We've travelled outside India together a couple of times, and have strengthened our bond on these trips. The first time we travelled together was to Amsterdam in 2008. Since then we've done lots of HIV conferences and even visited Thailand. We keep chatting on the flights, have lots of fun in the hotels. If you're with Laxmi, you'll never get bored. It's like 24/7 time pass with a whole lot of knowledge thrown in. There've been times when we've stayed up late into the night, chatting! Of course, the next morning is difficult because she refuses to wake up and get ready for the event we've come for!

The challenges we've faced as queer people have contributed greatly in forging our bond and further strengthening it. Laxmi comes from a culturally rich family—the Tripathis of Gorakhpur, Brahmins, have a very strong lineage and heritage. And for her to have identified as queer and broken out of that is remarkable. If my struggle has been intense because of the Rajput clan and my royal background, hers has been equally intense. And that's why even though she has a biological brother, Shashi, and they are very loving towards each other, I think she's closer to me as a brother and relates more to me. It's because her real brother is not queer—he's straight, with a family, in mainstream society, and he cannot understand her issues the way I can. I'm also extremely close to her biological family—Shashi had in fact travelled to Pune to attend the award ceremony where I was being felicitated when Laxmi couldn't make it. I always speak to her mother on the phone when we travel together. She's very sweet to me and I suspect is very fond of me. She still refers to Laxmi as a man though and sometimes I find that bewildering—'*Laxmi toh aaya nahi hai,*' or '*Laxmi toh bahut der se uthta hai,*' or '*Woh toh aisa hi hai bachpan se.*' If she has any complaints against Laxmi, she'll be sure to tell me, and if Laxmi is having problems with her mother or brother, she'll tell me to speak with them. It's like I'm the default mediator! I even find myself mediating on their personal family matters—but that's fine because I love all of them.

The story of how we came to be known as brother and sister is amusing, to say the least! Whenever Laxmi and I met at social events and functions, we always got along well. We noticed that some of our attributes matched, we have similar natures in some ways, and we were both physically similar as well—quite tall, and this was when Laxmi used to be very thin. As we came close to each other, we would marvel at how strongly we felt about each other. How could you just meet someone by absolute chance and develop such a close bond? So I once told her, 'Laxmi, don't you think we got separated in the Kumbh Mela? It's possible, no? That's why we feel this bond so strongly.' And she immediately said, 'Let's create this Kumbh Mela story!' After that, we would tell anyone and everyone we met that we were separated at birth during the Kumbh Mela. It was for a lark and we'd both have fun with the story and how we'd concocted it. Sometime ago, when the press had come to the fort in Rajpipla and Laxmi was staying with us as a guest, we told them that same story jokingly—and they printed it also! So it follows us around everywhere now.

When I came out as gay, when I finally gathered the courage to abandon the life of lies I was living and start living my own life, my parents disowned me. Laxmi stood by me in those difficult times. She called me up to say, '*Main hijron ki fauj le aaongi Rajpipla* (I'll bring an army of hijras to Rajpipla), don't worry. I'll tell the queen I'm the biggest queen over here. *Aapka raj mahal saare hijre capture kar lenge, toh kya karogi, maharani?* (If your royal fort is taken over by hijras, then what will you do, O queen?) Then the queen won't have any right to do or say anything to you. You don't need to worry about anything.' I can never forget how very supportive she was, how her strength and confidence were a boon for me when I was coming out. Of course I told her that I was handling the royal family, and the queen specifically, and I would let her know if I needed her help and the hijra fauj takeover!

Historically, in royal families, hijras were patronized by royalty and given positions of great honour; they had a respectable role to play. Whenever I'm called for press meets, I always speak about this fact. Nobody can say that India has never had transgenders or hijras, or that they are not part of our society—we have records of this in all royal families that depict, in detail, the close associations between royalty and hijras. Laxmi also takes pride in this fact, of my being part of a royal family. I always tell her, 'If you're my sister, then that makes you a princess.' She loves that of course.

I don't think we could have thought of a better relationship for each other and I will be her brother till the very end. She calls me *Bhai saa*—the traditional term of affection for brother in my native state—and I . . . Well I simply call her Laxmi. My sister, Laxmi.

RAJU'S MONOLOGUE

The phone rings. It is Urmila didi, my cousin who lives in Gorakhpur. She is crying. There's been a fight at home again, the same old domestic troubles that all married women seem to face, one way or another. And she's calling me. Like she did the last time. And the time before that.

I listen patiently and try and offer her sympathy, support—things she's deprived of, bereft of—because I do care and she knows that. We're very close, having grown up together in a way and just hearing my voice can calm her down. It's the same with Bindu didi, her sister. It's the kind of intimacy that brings us all to tears when we speak to each other after ages, and when they plead with me and call me 'Raju bhaiyya', I can't help but break down.

Raju lives and breathes inside me and no matter what I think or do or say, or how much I fight as an activist for transgenders' rights. Despite the breast implants that make me feel like a woman and my saris and my precious lipsticks, Raju will always live and breathe inside me. He refuses to leave, this oldest son of the Tripathi clan on whose shoulders rest innumerable family responsibilities. I could be applying my favourite mascara and getting ready to go out, and suddenly there he is—staring back at me in the mirror as I pause, brush in hand, and look back at him. Raju.

Sometimes he takes over too, when it is the need of the hour. He was there, putting on a brave show of masculinity when Papa was in abject pain from the cancer and suffering terribly. Making sure there was always enough money for everything, the treatment he required, the medicines he needed, all the financial support Papa was so dependent on. Papa, who had never asked anyone for anything all his life, and had lived his entire life righteously and with pride, his honour intact—a true head of the family who never had any of us wanting for anything, who toiled day and night for all of us, his family, for me. And when he was breathing his last, on his deathbed, Raju was by his side, he had to be. Papa had a blank look in his eyes for the longest time—pain can leave you so numb—but then he looked at me and I heard him say something. I heard the words in my head even though he did not mouth them. It was as if he was saying, 'I am going, Raju. As the eldest son,

RED LIPSTICK

now it's your responsibility to take care of this family.' I took Papa's hands in mine and nodded, tears in my eyes. Papa closed his eyes and drifted off, I am sure he found some peace in my acquiescence, some assurance that even though he was going away, everyone would be looked after.

He passed away soon after. But I could still hear him calling me. 'Raju!' To my father, my mother, and to many others who have known me since I was a child, like the people in my neighbourhood and colony, I still am and will always be Raju.

My sister Rukmini as well as my cousins Urmila and Bindu back in the village tie rakhis on my wrist, every year. When they did the thread ceremonies of their sons, which is a very significant milestone in a Brahmin boy's life, an important and sacred coming-of-age ritual, I went for it as a brother. I fulfilled all the responsibilities that befall an older brother as per tradition—from all the things that have to be bought, to being present in the puja, performing the ceremonies as per the officiating priest's directions.

Maintaining my relationship with them has been intensely crucial for me, and of course even more so for them. Life in Gorakhpur is still very orthodox and follows the same old system and culture—the old world and the values and systems that are thriving in most of India; it's not like the cities at all. So there is no place for a married woman to vent her true feelings, she is only meant to do her duty and respect her elders and all that. The only real space she has where she can be herself and speak about her problems and concerns, how she's feeling, is in her parents' home, her *maayka*—the only place where she can be free. Now imagine if their maayka is uncaring or doesn't wish to maintain the relationship, then these women have nowhere to go. I understand this about them, I sympathize with their pain. That's why they have kept in touch with me all these years, and continue to stay in touch—it's because I keep that relationship intact for them, and they know that in their parents' home, they at least have a brother who cares for them and will always care for them. When my father was alive, he maintained every single relationship in his family, no matter how difficult it was, and he kept them all in balance. After him, I have made sure that I have done the same. I know it is what he must have wanted, and as Raju, it is my duty to make sure Papa's last wishes come true.

As Raju, I can never let my mother and the spirit of my father down—they have always been there for me even when it was tough for them, even when our society would taunt them in ways unimaginable and painful to any parent. When I took the decision to not stay in a hijra ghetto and be available and accessible to my parents, a huge part of that call was because I wanted to be Raju for them. It is also because *they* wanted that and expected that—after all in our culture and society, there is no reason for a son to leave his parents' home ever, it is not considered a very respectable or desired move. When I became a hijra, my family did not understand why I was doing that, what it was that I was going through. As it is, I never told them directly—they found out one fine evening when they turned on the news and saw me speaking on behalf of hijras, as a hijra myself. I still remember that day like it was yesterday; I don't think it'll ever fade away from my mind. As part of the protests against Section 377, a meeting had been called at the Press Club in South Mumbai that was being attended by Ashok Row Kavi as well as some members of the hijra community. After the meeting, I was approached by several reporters and journalists looking for a sound byte or a comment. Until then, I had been living a secret life in a way—my parents weren't aware that I had inducted myself into the community. I remember Ashok cautioning me that if I were to appear on TV, there would be no going back, that my family would certainly come to know. But I didn't pay heed and went on to speak to the press. That night, all hell broke loose at home. When I entered the house, Mummy was beating her chest and wailing loudly as if someone had died. As for Papa, he was absolutely furious. I had never seen him like that. 'Why have you done this to us?' they kept on saying. There has been no precedent of anything like this in fourteen generations of Tripathis, I was told. On and on they went, about the family's good name, our standing in Gorakhpur, indeed all of Uttar Pradesh, our status as members of a high-caste clan, a Brahmin family. I could do nothing but listen for I knew then that Raju had failed them.

But even after all that, they did not turn against me. They could so easily have shunned me, which is the fate of most eunuchs in our country. But instead they chose the more difficult option: They wanted me to continue to live with them, as I was. I could be whoever I was, whoever I wanted to be—even if it meant being a hijra, if that's what made me most comfortable in my skin—but to them, I must stay and always remain Raju. This was never spelt out as such, but it was understood. Anyway, what could I possibly gain from causing them so much pain, if they had to let their Raju go away forever?

On the TV show *Sach Ka Saamna*, my father had declared in no uncertain terms that he considered me his son. 'As my eldest son, Laxmi Narayan is heir to my property in Mumbai and Uttar Pradesh,' he had said. 'My younger son, Shashi Narayan, is second to inherit.' When he was asked if he had ever thought about throwing me out of the house, he had responded, 'Why would I expel Laxmi from my family? I am his father, he is my responsibility. A hijra can be born to any family. If we shun them from our lives and homes, we leave them with no choice but to become beggars. I would never do that to someone in my family.' He always maintained that he had no right to interfere in his son's life.

Today, they have all accepted me as I am—our emotional bonding overrides everything. It's not about my identity and sexuality any more. What they see in me, how they recognize me, is most important to them. And to me. After I achieved so much fame, there has been more than a general acceptance in any case. Now I can say even my sisters' families in Gorakhpur are proud of me.

If Papa always saw me as Raju and only Raju— even when I went and initiated myself into the hijra community, even when I wore saris and make-up—who am I to question that? Who am I to decide how he sees me? I have no right. When I joined the hijras, it was Papa who had the second room at home taken off rent, so that I could continue to stay at home, as a hijra. I was once part of an unsavoury situation when my guru, Lata guru, tried to defame me. She called for a *chatai* meeting—it's like the panchayat wherein decisions relating to the community are made—and my father insisted that my mother go and attend the chatai to ensure that my guru and the community did not take any decisions that might ruin their child's life. No parent will ever say that—that yes, you should go to the *hijron ka panch*—but he did and he also instructed my mother to call him immediately if there were any issues. 'Nothing untoward should happen to Raju,' he told her. And my mother too, despite all that ghunghat business, really held her ground there. When it comes to her children, she is like a lioness protecting her cubs.

Papa would always be anxious and concerned about me. 'Where is Raju?', 'Did he eat something?', 'When will he come?' He was also very proud of me, praising me to the skies when talking about me. When I went to the UN—the first Indian transgender activist to do that—he said, 'Oh, see my child. Whatever else there is or anyone says, Raju has definitely made me proud.' 'My child is my child,' he would always say, 'and he will be my son, my Raju, till my last breath.'

And so it is that Raju must live. Always. I cherish him and nurture him, and keep him alive for Papa, for Mummy, for my sisters, for my brother, for my family. That moment when I look into the mirror and see him might seem aberrant for someone on the outside, but one thing is for sure: Raju is here to stay.

THE DESTROYER

The Transformer

·◇· Vidyut ·◇·

The journey was brutal, the results, glorious

You never forget your first real heartbreak. I met Jaspal through a common friend during my days as a model coordinator. Such a handsome Punjabi boy he was! My friend challenged me that I would never be able to snag him because he was completely straight and all that! But all the men I've met and slept with have always claimed that they are heterosexual—maybe it means they found the woman in me? It's fine with me, because it's what they want to relate to. For them, I was their woman, and who am I to judge? We have more than enough gods to judge us, so us mere mortals should just chill. Anyway, one dip in the Ganges will wipe away all my sins—that's what my religion has taught me. The rest is all bloody moralistic society.

So I accepted the challenge. The fact that Jaspal was so fuckable made it even more interesting! If a man can feel that way about a woman—that she's fuckable—I can also feel that way about a man. It was a case of challenge accepted and won! I won the bet because I slept with him on the first night we met. Done and dusted! But, of course, I fell hard for him—hook, line and sinker. And when I love, I love completely and madly. I cannot tame my love, I don't know how to temper it. I know only one way to love, it's who I am. I started living with him, it was my first live-in relationship, I didn't go back home for nights together and I would lie to my parents when they asked where I'd been.

But maybe I became overbearing for Jaspal. All he wanted was sex, ejaculation, and once that was done, he did not think of me until he was horny again. And soon enough he betrayed my trust. We had an understanding: He could see anybody else he wanted to, as long as he told me beforehand. But he didn't tell me and went ahead and dated my friend anyway. I confronted him and that's how it ended. We broke up on my birthday and all my friends remember that birthday as the funeral birthday. We were all crying together, my heart was in pieces. Eventually, the girl he had been dating also broke up with him. His circumstances turned for the worse and he left Mumbai and went back to his village. I don't think he even got a chance to complete his studies.

I spoke to him after years recently and we re-connected—it was strange. But Jaspal taught me a valuable lesson: Men are like tissue paper—use and throw. That's what I got out of that relationship. And that knowledge made me strong, and allowed me to flourish.

Listen, O Lord of the Meeting Rivers/Things Standing Shall Fall

It's a strange world where your own teacher, someone who has been a mentor to you, can turn against you. I've been told that the teacher–student relationship is of two kinds—in one the teacher is proud that the student has risen above him, and in the other, the teacher is resentful. Ashok Row Kavi, I would have to say, belongs to the latter category.

It was right after my class four final exams that I went in search of Ashok. I had been told that he 'works with men like me' and could help me. In those days, Ashok and his friends used to meet at Maheshwari Gardens, which was like the gay haven back then, where they would discuss issues concerning the community. So I went there and the moment I spotted the group, I felt so much better. They seemed like me, men who were effeminate. People probably called them by the same 'names' they hurled at me—'homo', *'mamu'*, *'chhakka'*. I approached the group and asked who Ashok Row Kavi was. He came up to me, affectionately patted my back, and asked me what I wanted. I introduced myself, telling Ashok everything about me. 'I am effeminate,' I began, 'and people tease me. I am also sexually attracted to men. Am I abnormal?' Ashok smiled and said, 'No, my child, you are absolutely normal. What is abnormal is the world around us.' He advised me to concentrate on my studies, to never give up dancing, and to meet him after I cleared my SSC exams. I looked up to him all my life, but years later, after I entered the social sector and started working, I think the rift started in his own mind, in his own thoughts.

Ashok never liked the fact that I called myself a hijra, that I claimed hijras are different from gay men, that we do not belong to the MSM category. I have always been emphatic in making this difference clear—MSM is a behavioural aspect, I do not belong to that group. I am a community, I am a hijra, a different being altogether. I am definitely *not* a man. But he never wanted to engage with that discussion, he always wanted us to be in that famous MSM chart he makes. And I told him, 'Ashok, who are you to decide we are men? Transgenders are different.' I think he may have started hating me then. It also had a lot to do with organizational social politics, and Mumbai is a completely political space when it comes to the social development sector in this arena. Maybe he wanted all the fame and he couldn't stand that I was getting so much attention. In a way, it's human nature—we all succumb to jealousy at times, but I was never envious of him. I sincerely only have respect for his contribution to the cause—I spoke very highly about his work on a TV programme because at the end of the day that's what the attention should be on—the larger cause, the *work*. But unfortunately, that's not how he views it. Ashok tried his best to throw me out of the social service sector. He tried to defame me, saying I had no capacity for real social work. But I proved him wrong by working in all capacities in every sphere of this movement, from women's policies to gay and lesbian rights to the problems of sex workers—I did it all, I was everywhere. I think he couldn't swallow that because he was always limited to one section and he never even wished to step outside of it—so my fame must have pinched him. But if you want to question a person, you can do it ideologically, for the work he or she does, but not on a personal level. Ashok attacked me even on that level. When my book *Me Hijra, Me Laxm*i came out, he wrote such a strange critique of it—extremely personal, scathing and very immature. *(Turn to 'For Your Eyes Only', page 195, for a citation of this review.)*

It was shocking to me that a person of his calibre could behave like that. He was my mentor, how could he just turn into a vicious enemy? I felt so hurt because I have never attacked anyone on a public forum and I never will—you just don't do that.

When I started the kinnar akhara, Ashok deliberately organized the CCM elections on the same date. I had called him up and requested him not to. 'Amma,' I had said, because that's what he's called, 'please postpone the dates, Amma.' But he did not. If he really had the heart of a mother, if he was truly 'Amma', things would have been very different. A mother is someone who forgives her child's mistakes, she does not strip her child naked in public—but that's exactly what Ashok did to me and he lost all my respect. After the akhara episode, he sent me all these emails that were completely personal attacks, some of them even mentioned my silicone implants, how I don't have real breasts—it was shocking behaviour. That's when I began to detest him too. Since then I have learnt that many other people have been on the receiving end of his back-biting and personal attacks. Shivananda Khan, Vijay Nair, Jasmeet Thakur, so many people!

The saddest part is that Ashok never grew out of the Humsafar Trust. For me, it was never only about

Astitva; the *community* is what is important and that should be the focus. For him, it's all about the trust and whether there are funds or not. This attitude of his has also caused serious harm in the social sphere. He has disappointed many people with his poor leadership, particularly with Section 377, which directly affects the gay community, his own community. Ashok could easily have been the best of leaders; he would have been worshipped at altars for eras to come if he could have, even for a moment, set aside his pettiness and viciousness and become involved in it thoroughly. But down the toilet it all went, otherwise we would have had a beautiful judgement there also.

I had stopped going to the Gay Pride march because of Ashok Row Kavi and the politics he played with me in Mumbai. But I started going to it again when it shifted to Delhi and because the lack of leadership for Section 377 is just too intense—there is nobody iconic. Leadership and activism cannot be confined indoors in offices and NGOs, they have to be demonstrated out on the streets. But when I started doing that, I came into the spotlight, I was noticed and respected. And he must have felt a further dilution of his power. Patriarchy doesn't leave you even when you're gay, does it? It only becomes about power. Like some of those transmen—women

LAXMI

who transition into men—and how they then go over the top with their power play and patriarchal politics.

I am nothing compared to Ashok Row Kavi, but it's so sad when you get scared of your own shadow, of your own people. You feel so insecure that you set about to damage your own children. How can you be insecure of your own?

But Ashok is the person solely responsible for diminishing Ashok's status in my life. He chose to do it, I did not. And since he's made that choice, I will respect it. There is an Urdu couplet I love—'*Tera taffagur tujhe mubarak, mujhe judaai ka gham nahi.*' I have outgrown him. I have moved on.

And from the Remains/Emerges the One Who Stands Tall

Can a six-year-old understand abuse? Comprehend the violence done to him? Can he ever really understand that he has been forced? What does it mean to be sexually abused at such a young age when you don't even know what abuse means? A child does not have the vocabulary of victimization handy and so he spends a large part of his life in denial of what has happened to him, never completely understanding it. Not knowing where to start.

You can't speak about consent in this context, because it is not even the right word—really, what consent would a child have to give?

The first time I was sexually abused was in our hometown, in Gorakhpur, where I had gone along with my family, to attend a wedding. I was a six-year-old boy who was weak, ill and feminine in demeanour, and that's what made me vulnerable. He was my first cousin—my father's elder brother's son, twenty-one years old. A sickly child, whose parents were slogging to keep him alive and well day and night, was whom he penetrated. I fainted the first time. The pain was so intense I felt something had ripped apart inside me, something was broken that could never be fixed. He went on raping me during the course of that wedding, and even brought in another cousin and some friends. I was in constant pain, there was a burning I can never describe and can never ever forget. Even as they would thrust inside me, they would whisper to me, 'You shouldn't tell anybody about this. You must promise.' See, because they were my own people, my own cousins, my family, I never thought they would do anything wrong to me, that they could ever dream of hurting me. So I never understood it as something wrong. But it caused me so much pain and confusion, I couldn't think straight. And because he was so close to us, my abuser was always in front of my eyes, even as I was growing up.

I never spoke to anyone about it. It was only much later in life, when I encountered sex and desire and understood what it was, that I realized that what had happened to me then was the worst wrong a human being could do to another human being, to a child. Once I did though, I was uncontrollable. I thirsted for revenge and became a vengeful bitch, devoid of remorse, guilt, repentance and shame. I was like the unbridled Ganges roaring down from Mount Kailash, with no Shiva to stem my flow. When I realized that I was exploited as a child because of my femininity, I decided to use exactly that—my femininity—to wreak revenge. And did I wreak revenge! I satiated myself with it. I exploited man after man, in all awareness, with complete deliberation. I went through all the men in my family, one by one, replacing my frustration and confusion with blinding rage and pure revenge sex. I forced them into my bed and wielded my femininity as a weapon—I would make them so bloody paralysed that they would submit themselves to me completely, losing all self-control, all sense of propriety or decorum. Their patriarchy crushed my femininity and now it was coming back to crush them, because these were all those 'straight' men with wives and children—bloody hypocrites. Indian men will actually fuck anything, but they are always in denial about it, because their masculinity would be questioned and patriarchy would suffer. I understood this about them because I was made to understand it, forced to— and I exploited it to my advantage.

I am the epitome of sluthood—I can be the ultimate seductress and I can also suddenly become other-worldly, divine and naive. I'm like a serpent, slippery. It's like I'm accessible, but I'm not available; it's irresistible, and that's what they all submitted to. It was empowering! I would tease them, make them want it, and then I would make it seem that I never wanted it in the first place. So many times I would just leave them in the middle of it all, with their throbbing erections aching for climax— the absolute humiliation for any man. I played my femininity so well that they got manipulated.

I remember when so many people in the family were speaking against me, against my decision to join the hijra clan, those who had slept with me, they kept their mouths shut. What could they say? I had shown them their place. Even if they tried, one look into my eyes would make them shut up. I could say to them, 'You're talking against me? The crease you'd left on my bedsheets is still there. The memory and mark of that love bite is still there.'

It was during my sister's marriage that I had the most intimate encounters. I enjoyed every second of pleasure then. Because it was *my* pleasure then, *my bloody pleasure*, not theirs to take at will. Whether they got pleasure out of it or not was not my concern. It was irrelevant to me. I was a lioness on a hunt. I didn't care how I slayed, and what I slayed. I had no regrets.

We all know that hijras become sex toys in a patriarchal society and for a long time I believed that too. I thought it might be a good way to be accepted in the mainstream. But then being a sex toy and playing the victim simultaneously simply did not work for me. When you know yourself so well, know what you're capable of, and do what you're doing with full awareness, you can't play that game. It is an art. Also, people who have been abused very young, they always wear it on their sleeve, bear it like a cross—'Oh, I was abused.' Sure, what happened is inhuman, and it shouldn't have. But I feel we must talk more about the strength of overcoming it. I have been abused, discarded, treated horribly, yet I'm strong. I do talk about my abuse, but only as history. Yet there are so many people who talk about their abuse all the time, but when they reach a position of superiority and strength, when they become successful in life, they end up abusing others weaker than them—knowingly or, at times, unknowingly—but they never talk about that. But if you did it, you must talk about it. Anyway, I just can't be a victim. I am a celebration, I feel, and that's the narrative I choose for my story.

The guy who abused me is no longer alive—he died of HIV, a very painful, dreadful death; it was his karma. But when I grew up, I even forced him to have sex with me—I just caught him and flung him on to my bed and then I walked out halfway, leaving him powerless. I made out with somebody else while he was watching—yes, I did that too. Sex became my personal power tool, just like, I would imagine, it was Cleopatra's and Helen of Troy's. It was like my *cheer haran* had already happened, but I created my own Mahabharata, I took my revenge. This Draupadi didn't wait for Arjuna or Bheem to avenge her, so she could wash her hair in Duhshasana's blood and tie it up. She took matters in her own hands.

I never stopped to think about it, if what I was doing was right or wrong. I took the decision that I thought was right then, and I went with it. It was a conscious decision. And even today when I look back, I don't regret a single moment.

To see a hunk of a man helpless, with absolutely no control on himself—to strip him naked, to order him to strip naked—is a very powerful thing. I have never allowed a man in my bed with clothes on. You want to know something about men? Tell the man to strip naked, look him up and down and then bed him. He will never raise his head in front of a woman who does that. Nudity is simply not very normal for Indian men. Indian men are not comfortable in their own skins, they are not used to seeing themselves naked. Traditionally, they would even keep their underwear on while taking baths—it's in our culture. Even with their lovers and wives, they never strip naked completely before having sex—that erotic sense is just not there. So if you ask them to do that, it makes them completely helpless.

This gave me power and an incredible attitude towards men and sex. When men give so much attitude about their penises, I always say, '*Koi top toh nahi leke ghoom raha, na* (It's not like you're walking around with a cannon in your pants). It's one dick and two testicles. And it's not going to be a bucket of anything—it's like one tablespoon of cum. You'll squirt it on to my body, and it'll get recreated in you. So shut up.' When men would tease me about being a hijra, I would walk up to them and say, 'I know that your dick is not even bigger than your nose. So shut up.' This one time, there was this man who was desperate to sleep with me. He was a very good-looking man, but I didn't want to. So I told him, 'Have you seen the Mahalaxmi Race Course?' He said, 'Yes, of course.' So I said, 'My whole body is the Mahalaxmi Race Course. *Tere jaise kitne ghode daude hain, aur daud ke mar chuke hain* (Several horses like you have galloped across and died). What's the big deal? Get lost.'

My abuse and what came after it gave me this attitude, made me like this and talk like this. Yes, it came out of something that was not nice. My abusers introduced me to something that I should not have learnt then. And when I understood it and understood the pleasure of it, then who would fulfil my desires? It was their responsibility. They were family after all. And I have a family full of handsome hunks—so it was beautiful incest. Like King George V with all his wives and all that incest. Cousins, uncles, brother-in-law's brothers—I spared none.

THE LOVE MONOLOGUE

·◈· Like any hot-blooded woman/
I have simply wanted an object to crave ·◈·

Alanis Morissette, 'Uninvited'

The year I went on the school trip to Matheran, in 1992, was when he was born. And twenty years later, 23 April 2012, is when we met and we've been together ever since—my longest-lasting relationship with a man. Viki Thomas. The love of my life. The man to whom I have completely surrendered, the only man who rules over me, my heart, my body and my will. The man who has absolutely overpowered me and made me a woman. I gave myself to him the very first day we met—I have never ever done that, slept with a man I just met, except to win a bet. I don't know why, but I was just drawn to him.

Ours is a Facebook love—he sent me a message and I responded seeing how macho he looked. Of course I didn't know then he was a twenty-year-old kid! He told me he was twenty-nine! After some initial flirting, we finally met—he came to my house and I took him along to an event I had to attend in the evening. It was the tenth anniversary celebration of the Anaam Prem organization, which brings together dharma gurus from various religious orders every Mahavir Jayanti, who then relate stories of kinnars from different traditions, and organize cultural programmes. My mother was with us too; after the event, I sent her back home and Viki and I went for dinner. That night, we slept together. I felt an immediate spark, an instant connect with him. I've had so many lovers, so many sexual encounters and conquests, but never have I felt that I want this person to stay with me, forever. If anything, I was always the kind who wanted the person out of my bed and my life by the morning. But with Viki, it was strange. And strangely beautiful. The very next day I fed him with my hands and he had tears in his eyes. 'Nobody has ever fed me like this,' he said. We started talking and he began telling me, much to his own surprise, about losing his mother, how she had died some years ago, how he missed her, and how he felt at times that he had nowhere to go, nobody to guide him. I don't think he had ever spoken about all that to anyone, he had probably not even articulated it to himself. I suddenly felt responsible for the boy; I thought I could be the anchor for his lost, unmoored soul—I wanted to be that anchor for him, a safe haven, a refuge. I don't usually cook, I don't care for it much, but for him, I cook too. I make really delicious mutton keema, which he loves.

And I feel that responsibility till date. Just as I do for my family—be it my own biological family, my mother, my sisters, my brother, or my extended family, my chelas, my community. I strongly feel that Viki has come to me because I am responsible for him—that's how it was meant to be. It was in his destiny and mine too.

Viki is like a child because his childhood was destroyed. There's so much that cannot be mended when that happens to you. My childhood was destroyed too, but I was never in want of parental love and that makes a huge difference. Viki's father remarried and after his stepmother arrived, the strongest emotion that Viki felt was the need to escape. He started staying out all day, all night, and would rarely go back home. A sense of place, what we call and take for granted as home, was never available to him even at a young age.

I don't know whether my understanding of his situation is right or wrong, but this is my perception of him and how he is, how he feels, the way he is today. That's why when I ask him where he is, it irritates him no end, because nobody in his life has ever asked him these questions and he feels he's not answerable to anyone. But families always ask you these questions, those who care about you will ask you these things.

We have extremely intense fights all the time, but I always try and see things from his point of view and am usually the one to make amends and make up. *Ek ko udhedna aata hai, toh doosre ko bunna aana chahiye* (If one unravels the relationship, the other should know how to weave it back)—I always say. Most of our arguments have to do with my family, with whom Viki has a love–hate relationship. The tiniest of matters hurt him sometimes, something inconsequential that someone said, my mother's dig about his eating habits, for instance, but he'll take it to heart. My family too doesn't understand him at times. My mother feels that ever since he has come into my life, my own family has become less important to me, that somehow I care less for her. But that's not true. It's just that they've never seen me fall for a man so hard, and they don't know how to deal with it. Almost everyone thought Viki would be just a phase in my life—temporary, transient—but he seems to be in a permanent status with me, and that can be hard to comprehend for someone who has known me all my life. Everyone has a vested interest in keeping Laxmi close, I know that. That's why I am the centre of so many worlds. But in Viki I have found a centre for *my* world. That's the problem—that the centre of my world is a person, and it has led to a whole lot of insecurity. Till just a few years ago, nobody could believe that I could get so serious about a man! If someone had told me that, even I wouldn't have believed it; I would've waved him away and laughed it off!

The emptiness in my life with the passing away of my father was definitely one reason I felt this pull so strongly. Papa's absence brought Viki close to me. Everyone knows that a woman searches for her father in her companion, her spouse must be a reflection of her creator, her father, and I was very lonely when Viki arrived. I was doing great otherwise, I was famous, I had achieved a lot, but I was very lonely. I think that made me feel ready for a real relationship as well. Now I can say that he's my man, he owns me. For the first time in my life I can say that—that a man owns me. He's made me a woman. If I don't talk to him, I feel uneasy. The thought of losing him drives me nuts. I have cried for him millions of times, I cry for him at the drop of a hat. Isn't that what women in serious relationships do?

He's a kid, but he's so intense—if I look at someone a little longer than usual, then he'll shout at me, 'You don't know who you are. You can't behave this way.' He's always worried about my character; he doesn't want anybody to have a chance to assassinate it. 'Don't give them an opportunity,' he keeps telling me. He really takes care of me as well. He makes sure I stay healthy, pesters me not to brush my teeth with tobacco, not to drink too much. He always says, 'If something happens to you, it'll affect me also.' He quit smoking for me, because I have asthma. I changed for him too. I never used to care about my boyfriends earlier, but he made me realize that he could become like sand in my hand and trickle out any time, and so I should really care about my relationship with him, work on it. He has such absolute control over me . . . I have never felt like that with a man—that I have lost all control, that I'm not the one in-charge. He acts very patriarchal at times, like when he doesn't want me to wear saris. 'When you wear saris', he says, 'even those who might not notice you, will turn their heads and glance, or even stare at you. Why don't you wear something else? How about a Punjabi suit?' He also discourages me from wearing too much make-up, and he'll always tell me that he prefers me sans make-up. And of course I like it a lot when he acts that way, who wouldn't? Any woman who says she doesn't like it when her man is being possessive about her, is downright lying, she can never deny the pleasure she gets when her man behaves that way.

Sometimes I feel angry and I wonder if I'm losing my freedom, but then I let it go. After all, I consider him my husband now. I've stopped calling him my boyfriend and I even introduce him as my husband to everyone now, wherever we go and to everyone we meet.

Viki is very immature, he's only twenty-three; he needs to experience a lot more to discern more. I also feel I try and fill that gap for him, because I think he needs the right direction too. Sometimes he says that he'll leave his father for me, because his father, an orthodox Christian, will never accept our relationship. But I always tell him, 'No, Viki, that's not right. Life is not about breaking relationships. We have to keep mending them if there are cracks, apply the ointment and rejuvenate them.' With a damaged childhood behind him, Viki has not grown in that sense. After all, there are some things that can only be taught by a mother. He has to create his own self now, and he has been putting in a lot of effort to that end. I'll be by his side to make sure he has all the support he needs.

He also acts very childish at times—maybe we were all like that at twenty-three? Of course, I never had a childhood, it was snatched away from me. The few early years I had were totally immersed in sickness—from typhoid to pneumonia to malaria, I had them all and, sometimes, all at once too! But Viki—he'll at times behave in a moody manner in public, which leaves me embarrassed. Just the other day, we were having dinner with Shobha Ojha, president of the All India Mahila Congress. Shobha had decided to cook for us herself, and Viki had told her the kind of daal he wanted to eat—he gave her very specific instructions—but when it arrived on the table, he didn't eat even a morsel, saying he was not hungry! I know he didn't do that deliberately, we had all had a lot of snacks and small eats by then, so he was truly not hungry—none of us were, but we all took small portions, because you just can't behave like that at a social dinner! But Viki doesn't fathom all this and as of now, doesn't even want to.

At times, he'll resent that I get so many phone calls. I'm a celebrity, I'm famous, and my work is in the social sector, so that's bound to happen. I have a network of friends and relationships I have to maintain—so many times people find out your numbers even when you haven't shared them yourself. Occasionally, when Viki has answered my phone, he's been nasty to people, abusive even. As a result I have lost friends and acquaintances. There's an unnecessary aggression in him, which I guess is natural for his age. It's what led to an ugly encounter between us also. We were on a holiday in the hills and Viki was driving and we were having an argument, as always! He kept telling me to keep quiet because it was distracting him and it would be dangerous since we were on tricky terrain where even a tiny error could cost us our lives. But I was furious, and anyway when I get emotional, there's no stopping me. So I kept on arguing and his temper continued to mount. And then suddenly, in a flash, Viki hit me with the back of his hand—he works out and so is very strong—it was a powerful blow. I was stunned into silence and absolutely shocked at this behaviour, but I think Viki was too. He immediately started apologizing, it was as if he couldn't believe what he had just done. He kept telling me how he didn't mean to, and it was a reflex action of sorts because he was feeling so paranoid about driving and was really afraid he would get us into an accident. I have forgiven him since, but it has disfigured my nose. This episode has led a lot of people to mistrust Viki and even alienate him. They have warned me against him again and again, but I feel Viki will get over this phase also. He'll live and learn, and I am willing to give him time.

When he was in hospital for a few days, I was by his bedside the whole time. He was in tears because he never thought he could be so important to someone. He makes me feel responsible; I have never felt that way about anyone. Men have always had to adjust to my whims and fancies but for the first time in my life, I am the one doing the adjusting, changing anything and everything so that his emotions are not disturbed. Maybe this is what unconditional love is? I also find myself thinking about how I'll break if he ever leaves me. I have only negative thoughts in my head then. I start wondering which of my enemies sent him into my life, who is trying to break my emotional independence. Because now I'm so bound to one soul that my emotional dependence on that soul is absolute.

Whenever I imagine a groom's face, I can only see Viki's. I don't know if he'll have me, but that's one dream I have—of getting married. Of course, I'll make sure the dream comes true anyway, Viki or no Viki, even if I have to get a husband on payment, on a contract marriage for a month, and then get divorced later—but I will live that dream of getting married. I see my wedding as any other girl sees it. As a woman, I want it like any other woman. I have seen so many weddings in my family— my own sister's—and I have desires too. Just as I have tried to fulfil so many of my life's dreams, I will try to fulfil this one too. I firmly believe I am the monitor of my own dreams—god makes you dream so you can strive to realize them, not so you can keep hoping and praying that *He'll* make them come true one day! And my wedding day will be absolute dhamaal. There will be such great splendour. It'll be bloody hijrotic.

You can never gauge the other person's love for you, even in a husband–wife relationship, can you? And so I can never truly speak for Viki and his feelings for me, even though I do feel that he will never disown me. But for me, I know my love is true. If he leaves me, I will crumble completely, I will be destroyed. I'll topple from this pedestal that I feel I am standing on today, and be lying in the dust, at least on the inside. But for now, I'm enjoying the moment. And I know for sure that till his last breath, he will know that somebody loved him so deeply—that I'm certain of.

At times when Viki treats me badly I feel like it is my own doing. My karma is coming back to me. I have treated thousands of hearts this way and worse, played games, played with emotions, and so this is what I deserve. I am experiencing it all with Viki because he brings out only the woman in me—I can do anything to keep my man happy and that is a very powerful feeling, it can drive you to extremes.

I understand it now—how, to keep her husband happy, the woman will go to any lengths. How she'll sacrifice. How she'll become secondary in her own life, in her own eyes, with her own self. That person becomes your priority . . . And does he really value that, you wonder? Can he ever value that? Is it even possible, because the woman, after all, is doing it to her own self.

MANTHAN: THE CHURNING
OF LAXMI

·◇· Sometimes I just want to disown everything and everyone
I want to disown Laxmi, whoever she is
And just vanish . . . ·◇·

It is said that when the goddess cannot take it any more, when the pressures of being Goddess Laxmi overpower her forbearance, overwhelm her courage, bring her to breaking point, so much so that she is unable to recognize even her own self, Laxmi disappears.

She ups and leaves. As simple as that.

Indra sits there on his throne, resplendent one minute—living life to the hilt, a committed aesthete, soaking in all kinds of pleasures like a hedonist—and forlorn the next—because what is life without Laxmi?

Laxmi wants to vanish, she wants to go as far away as possible from this world of materialism and relationships, of wanting and craving, of granting wishes and being taken for granted, this world of talk-talk, all sound and fury. She wishes never to be found. Nothingness is her new ambition, a goal that seems achievable, a welcome end to it all.

And so it is that Laxmi dissolves herself into the ocean of milk, lost to Indra and his ilk forever. She submerges herself, going deep down where she can never be found. Oblivion can be bliss too, she learns.

> *But I have responsibilities*
> *Laxmi is not alone now*
> *Laxmi is in the midst of so many people*
> *And I have taken it all upon myself . . .*

But it is not meant to be.

The cycle turns, the ocean churns.

With Mandara as the staff, Kurma as the base, and Vasuki as the rope, the churning begins, Devas on one side and Asuras on the other.

It is inevitable that Laxmi emerge eventually. It is written in the books, the desperation of those seeking her is too powerful, it creates friction that she is bound to respond to. And so it is that she rises slowly but surely, and reappears in the world. Formed and shaped again by the need of those around her, who crave her, desire her and require her to sustain their lives and themselves. Her chosen silence and preferred state of retirement rendered inconsequential and shattered by this churning that is constant. A relentless *manthan*.

My family depends on me entirely
My mother, my brother, all look up to me
I cannot not *be there for them*
I cannot be anything but strong in front of them
And for them . . .
When I cry, I make sure the door is closed tight . . .

Laxmi is exhausted. A lifetime of being Indra's Sachi, of ensuring that he is never in want of anything, that he can bathe and relax in a fountain of plenitude for eternity has sapped the energy out of her. If she closes her eyes, she can still see Rishi Durvasa and his offerings of beautiful lotuses, pink and perfect, and his hot hot rage when Indra, too wrapped up in himself and his own pleasure, disrespected them. 'Why is it,' she wonders, for the millionth time, 'that he takes everything for granted, again and again? Why does he take me for granted each and every time?'

Laxmi has no answers, she only knows that her own divine energy is failing her yet again. And that she must disappear, vanish, yet again. The ocean of milk is waiting for the final embrace. Or what seems, at least, like the very last embrace.

Wanting to vanish is one fantasy I can never fulfil
Otherwise I have lived all my fantasies . . .

And once again, she submerges herself in the ocean. Longing for a state of silence, for a new way of life, one that is bereft of all the hankering and people's wants and needs and demands. But this is a dance, she knows it even then, an eternal, self-perpetuating waltz with the same cast of characters—the ocean, the Asuras, the Devas—over and over again.

Once again, the manthan begins, the tension develops and mounts, and the inevitable happens yet again: Laxmi rises to the occasion.

And once again, she puts her game face on.

For Your Eyes Only

I'd like to share with my readers the 'critique' that Ashok Row Kavi wrote of my first book, *Me Hijra, Me Laxmi*—which was so unexpected, for I consider him my mentor and indeed someone who helped me see myself with self-confidence. I can handle critiques, I have no issues if someone flags my flaws as a public personality and had what he had written been constructive criticism, I would have taken it in my stride. Not only that, I would have tried to correct myself as well. But his entire critique was a personal rant, an attack on me personally, which was uncalled for and severely unprofessional. That is not done.

I am citing it here: 'Fables and Half-truths: Autobiography of a Hijra', (*Hindustan Times,* 27 April 2015)—so that my readers may understand where I'm coming from.

As I said earlier—and this is something I've always maintained—I am, first and foremost, an activist, and I will always be one; it is my strongest, truest personal identity. I feel it is in my genes, in a way, because my dear father was also always clued into the needs of his fellow human beings and in his work too, at the factory, he became a union leader to be able to give voice to the rights of the workers. I know that you have to ask for your rights, you have to demand them, again and again and again. You have to be out on the streets, you have to be visible, you have to make noise. But there's more to activism than just making noise—there's also much thought, discussion, brainstorming with the policy-makers, the ones who care, and a whole lot of advocacy. I make sure I'm spearheading all these aspects of activism, and that I stay involved. When I don't understand things myself, I reach out for help—I have no shame in doing that because you only learn when you ask questions. That's what makes a true activist.

To this end, I was the intervenor in the matter of the *National Legal Services Authority* versus *Union of India and Others case in the Supreme Court*, which ultimately met with a favourable verdict.

The following excerpt, quoted verbatim, is from the release on the Lawyers Collective official website:*

In a case that has the potential to break the binary gender norms of male and female in law and administrative practices in the country, the Supreme Court on 29th October, 2013 reserved its judgment on the question of recognition of identity of transgender persons in India. The Division Bench of Justice K.S. Radhakrishnan and Justice A.K. Sikri was hearing a public interest litigation, *National Legal Services Authority* (NALSA) *v. Union of India & Ors.* (Writ Petition [Civil] No. 400 of 2012) filed in October, 2012. The petition sought several directions from the Court, including granting of equal rights and protection to transgender persons; inclusion of a third category in recording one's sex/gender in identity documents like the election card, passport, driving license and ration card; and for admission in educational institutions, hospitals, access to toilets, amongst others.

Senior Advocate and Director, Lawyers Collective, Mr. Anand Grover appeared on behalf of Laxmi

---

* lawyerscollective.org

Narayan Tripathi, a famous *hijra* activist, and an intervener in the matter. Addressing the Bench on the questions raised in the Petition, Mr. Grover pointed out that gender is now understood as a continuum or a range, which is not restricted to the binary of male and female gender alone and which may be different from a person's biological sex. A person may identify in the gender, which does not correspond with the sex assigned at birth, for example, a person, who is assigned female sex at birth, may identify as male or may identify as transgender, that is, other than male or female.

Mr. Grover argued that a person's sense or experience of gender is integral to their core personality and their sense of being. Everyone has a right to be recognised in her chosen gender. This right lies at the heart of personal autonomy and freedom of persons. He further argued that recognition of gender identity should not be dependent on medical requirements, that is, one should not be required to undergo any medical procedure like hormonal therapy or sex reassignment surgery (SRS), in order to get legal recognition. At the same time, if one wishes to undergo any medical procedure, one should have access to free and quality health services, including SRS in public hospitals.

Reading Articles 14 and 15 (equality and non-discrimination), 19 (fundamental freedoms) and 21 (right to life) together, Mr. Grover submitted that the State has a duty to recognise the self-identified gender of all persons and should take necessary legal and administrative steps to accord such recognition in all identity documents, whether issued by the State or private entities and which indicate a person's sex/gender, including birth certificates, educational certificate, passport, ration card and driving license. He further argued that the Constitution itself had recognised gender, which was included in the term 'sex' used in Article 15. He thus noted that the constitutional guarantee of equality applies to all and no one can be discriminated by the State on the ground of 'gender identity' under Article 15.

Mr. Grover asserted that there can be no justification for the State not recognising gender identities, other than male and female, especially when India has a rich tradition of persons who identify as the third gender. He traced the history of third gender identity to ancient religious and other texts and referred to the prominent role of the *Hijra* community in the royal courts of the Mughal rulers. However, the British criminalised the entire class of *hijras* in the 19th century, by categorizing them as a 'criminal tribe' and denuding them of their civil rights. The impact of criminalisation is still felt in many local laws even today, for instance, Section 36A was introduced in 2012 in *the* Karnataka Police Act, *1964,* which provides for 'registration and surveillance of Hijras who indulged in kidnapping of children, unnatural offences and offences of this nature.'

The Union of India, through the Ministry of Social Justice and Empowerment (MOSJE), submitted they were in principle in agreement with the submissions pertaining to the recognition of transgender persons in law and that they have set up an expert committee on the issues relating to transgender persons and would take into account all the concerns raised by the Petitioner and the Interveners.

I have also been fighting with all my will and might towards the eradication of the severely outdated Section 377, a matter that received a landmark judgement in the Delhi High Court, and is now pending decision in the Supreme Court.

The following excerpt is a summary of the status of the case against Section 377, from the official Lawyers Collective official website[†]:

Sec 377—Sec 377 of the Indian Penal Code (IPC), 1860, enacted by the British colonial regime to criminalise 'carnal intercourse against the order of nature', reads thus: 377—Unnatural Offences— Whoever voluntarily has carnal intercourse against the order of nature with any man, woman or animal, shall be punished with imprisonment for life, or with imprisonment of either description for a term which may extend to ten years, and shall also be liable to fine.'

Lacking precise definition, Section 377 became subject to varied judicial interpretation over the years. Initially covering only anal sex, it later included oral sex and still later, read to cover penile penetration of other artificial orifices like between the thighs or folded palms. The law made consent and age of the person irrelevant by imposing a blanket prohibition on all penile-non-vaginal sexual acts under the vague rubric of 'unnatural offences'.

[†] lawyerscollective.org

Though ostensibly applicable to heterosexuals and homosexuals, Section 377 acted as a complete prohibition on the penetrative sexual acts engaged in by homosexual men, thereby criminalising their sexual expression and identity. Besides, the society too identified the proscribed acts with the homosexual men, and the criminalisation had a severe impact on their dignity and self-worth. Section 377 was used as a tool by the police to harass, extort and blackmail homosexual men and prevented them from seeking legal protection from violence; for fear that they would themselves be penalised for sodomy. The stigma and prejudice created and perpetuated a culture of silence around homosexuality and resulted in denial and rejection at home along with discrimination in workplaces and public spaces.

The *Naz Foundation (India) Trust*, a Delhi-based non-governmental organization and working in the field of HIV prevention amongst homosexuals and other men having sex with men (MSM), realised that Section 377, IPC constituted one of the biggest impediments in access to health services for MSM. MSM remained a hidden population due to fear of prosecution under the law. Through its interactions with clients, Naz Foundation became acutely aware of the disproportionate and invidious impact of Section 377 on homosexuals.

In 2001, Lawyers Collective, on behalf of *Naz Foundation (India) Trust*, filed a writ petition in Delhi High Court challenging the constitutionality of Section 377 on grounds of violation of right to privacy, dignity and health under Article 21, equal protection of law and non-discrimination under Articles 14 and 15 and freedom of expression under Article 19 of the Constitution. Notice was issued to Union of India in 2002 and the Attorney General was asked to appear. The Ministry of Home Affairs filed an affidavit opposing the petition in September, 2003. The petition was dismissed by the High Court on 02.09.2004 for lack of cause of action as no prosecution was pending against the petitioner.

The Petitioner filed a review petition (RP 384/2004) in the High Court against the order of dismissal but that too was dismissed on 03.11.2004. Aggrieved by the same, the Petitioner filed a Special Leave to Appeal (C.N. 7217-18/2005) in the Supreme Court of India in 2005. On 03.02.2006, the Supreme Court passed an order holding that '*the matter does require consideration and is not of a nature which could have been dismissed on the ground afore-stated*'. Remitting the matter back to the High Court of Delhi to be decided on merits, the Supreme Court set aside the said order of the High Court. Subsequently, the Ministry of Health and Family Welfare through National AIDS Control Organisation (NACO) submitted an affidavit in support of the petition in the High Court contending that Section 377 acted as an impediment to HIV prevention efforts in July, 2006.

Thereafter, the final arguments in the matter ensued in November, 2008 before the division bench of Chief Justice of Delhi High Court A.P. Shah and Justice S. Muralidhar.

On 02.07.2009, the Delhi High Court passed a landmark judgment holding Section 377 to be violative of Articles 21, 14 and 15 of the Constitution, insofar as it criminalised consensual sexual acts of adults in private.

Following the High Court decision, 15 Special Leave Petitions (SLPs) were filed in the Supreme Court appealing against the said decision on behalf of mostly faith-based and religious groups from all parts of India. 7 intervention applications (I.A.s) were also filed; out of which, 5 I.A.s were in support of the High Court judgment while 2 I.A.s were against the decision. Importantly, the Union of India did not appeal against the judgment and the Supreme Court too did not grant a stay on the operation of the same. In February, 2012, final arguments began in this matter before the division bench of Justice G.S. Singhvi and Justice S.J. Mukhopadhyay and continued till the end of March, 2012. Mr. Anand Grover, Senior Advocate and Director, Lawyers Collective argued on behalf of Naz Foundation (India) Trust and defended the Delhi High Court decision. The judgment is currently awaited.

On 29 June 2016, the Supreme Court referred a petition against Section 377 filed for the first time by five LGBT celebrities—chef and restaurateur Ritu Dalmia, owner of the Neemrana chain of hotels Aman Nath, dancer Navtej Singh Johar, senior journalist Sunil Mehra, and businesswoman Ayesha Kapur—to a constitution bench.

✂ Postscript by Hoshang Merchant ✂

All angst is linguistic. So is Laxmi's angst and that of others of her ilk. There is no word in Indian languages for 'homosexual'. The concept did *not* exist before British India. So Laxmi calls herself a 'hijra' (eunuch), concocts a new etymology ('pure soul') and saves 'herself' from castration.

Laxmi is not subversive enough because she stays within the family. In this she joins the self-declared gay poet Vikram Seth and the characters in Mahesh Dattani's gay farces and Onir's in *My Brother Nikhil* (note, 'brother', *not* 'lover').

The gender-bending is hilarious. Social workers Meera and Anjali become her 'husbands from a past life.' (Masculine women are male; feminine men 'female' to Laxmi and rightly so.) They give her a few insights: How maybe, we're all trans (that is, transsexual, mentally). How women have to renegotiate their territories among male-dominated groups (eunuchism redefines patriarchy). How using 'karma' is a bad idea because it makes gays, women, Dalits, all oppressed groups responsible for their fate (of being born so) which isn't really so.

But the great battle from the Suez to Sumatra today (with India thrown in) is between tradition and modernity. The fact is Laxmi, like all of us, negotiates modernity through tradition.

But does she lapse into being a doormat of a 'wife' at thirty-seven to a twenty-year-old? That is, she succumbs to her 'fate' as a masochist. God help her! And us. Yes, Meena Kumari wins yet again. But should we let her? That said, Laxmi, an object of great envy, has done great work for her ilk all the way up to the UN. Be prepared to see her in Parliament. Amen!

It's amazing to see Laxmi's encounter with the Dalit minister for women's welfare in Maharashtra who helps Laxmi include women and hijras among the socially deprived groups worthy of receiving welfare. She is one among a slew of bureaucrats and police officers (mostly Brahmin). That Laxmi is born Brahmin has helped just as my being Parsi (and fair-skinned) has helped me further my gay liberation agenda, relatively unscathed.

I read through this manuscript straight for five hours, so gripping it is. Laxmi is fascinating because like the brother and sister in Shakespeare's *Twelfth Night* we have not only exchanged our clothes with her, we, Laxmi and all of us, have also exchanged our souls. She, like an impossible character in Shakespeare, has entered our lives and our dreams.

Hyderabad   Hoshang Merchant
15 July 2016

❦ The Way We Are, the Way We Love: Writer's Note and Acknowledgements ❦

If you ask a man when it was that he began to really think of himself as a man, chances are he'll have a few stories to tell you, mostly along the lines of what his parents told him, or what the world at large said to him every single day, what sorts of birthday presents he got, the kinds of clothes he wore, even the water bottles he'd carry to school!

If you dig deep, you'll realize that how he essentially came to that rock-solid understanding of his gender was largely shaped by an understanding of what (or who) he was definitely not (thank god!)—a woman.

When you ask a woman the same question, you'll discover the true meaning of education-by-suggestion.

A lifetime of hints, cajoling, coaxing, nagging, pushing (and shoving if needed) to help her arrive at the same place she's been at for centuries—cooking, caring, nurturing, all very naturally. The woman too learns about her gender in relation to who she can (unfortunately) never be—a man.

It says something about us as a culture, as a race, when we build the blocks of our own identities and selves through the sheer politics of othering. That our genders are mere socio-biological constructs, which have been conveniently frozen in time, following rules and codes that date back to the prehistoric era when the males of the tribes were going out into the wild, hunting and gathering, and the females were back in the caves, birthing and nursing. When, as they like to say, men were men, and women, women.

That we then hang our sexualities on to these staid pegs is an idea so subhuman it would be ridiculous and hilarious if we didn't know it as the world's truth. And the only truth. Which is what makes it a sheer and utter tragedy. Surely, we should know better than that. Because we have the cerebral and intellectual power to be able to distinguish the biological make-up of a person—that includes genitals, chromosomes, secondary sexual features—from one's gender attributes—that would encompass a self-image, and a psychological or emotional sense of sexual identity.

Besides, can something as life-altering and earth-shattering as human sexual desire really function on autopilot mode? Even if we can box in gender, can our sexualities really ever be subsumed within boxes?

Wither and choke in a straitjacket, won't you, as opposed to running wild and free?

If we recognize gender as fluid, an emotion at best—distance ourselves and our identities from all the conditioning—then surely we'll find sexuality breathing too. And frolicking.

But that's not the world we live in. Choosing to think about all this is an ask we're not prepared to engage with. Because boxes are neat, boxes are practical, and they save us time. If you are born in a certain gender, then you must adapt to the ascribed gender behaviour, so we can all relate well to one another—convenience over self-expression, any day, it seems. Especially if you'd like to be perceived as 'normal', because the non-conformists make us really uncomfortable.

Something Laxmi knows more than a thing or two about.

Laxmi Narayan Tripathi, born a biological male, always felt more at home mirroring feminine behaviour.

Crippled with uncertainty, she went through a range of identities in her yearning to find one that fit—a journey explored in the 'Red Lipstick Monologue' that opens this book—before finally aligning herself with the oldest transgender community in the world—the hijras. A believer of free will, Laxmi decided to forgo castration or what the hijras call 'nirvana', and what the fashionable world has now termed 'gender-confirmation surgery' (moving on from 'gender-reassignment'), thanks to the likes of Caitlyn Jenner. Although I suspect that family and social standing, which mean the world to Laxmi, might have had something to do with this decision as well.

Besides, Lady Gaga telling us that it's all good because 'Baby, I was born this way' is a world far away from the reality of mainstream India. A world where questions like 'What will the neighbours say?' still have considerable weight.

When I first met Laxmi, she told me she wanted to write a book about dicks. Ice smashed (because when someone tells you something like that, it's not merely broken), we started talking. We met several times during the course of the making of this book, often in her pet Karol Bagh motel in Delhi, where she would place room service orders of hot pakoras and adrak chai, and turn from being confessor to agony aunt in the span of one day. At times, I would find her in a deeply introspective frame of mind, and she was often, if not always, defiant and supremely provocative. There were several moments of performance—Laxmi loves her tamasha. 'Men are intriguing things,' she mumbled one evening as she got ready for a night out, working the felt tip of the raven-black liner on her eyes, crafting intricate swooshes. 'A woman can only enjoy her own femininity if a man appreciates it. So men and women—it's a wonderful mix. But that's where I come in between—standing tall, imposing, at 5'11", not knowing where I am, who I am. And getting into that battle . . .'

There are days when she's by herself at home in Thane, Mumbai, when she grapples with intensely painful questions. Having just received herself 'a parcel for Laxmi' from someone who didn't recognize her, she mulls, 'Am I a woman? I am not. But I'm not a man . . .' On good days, she convinces herself, 'I find gender so unromantic, such an artificial imposition assigned to you based on your body parts. Can a dick or a pussy define me? Please! So fuck it.' Her resolution comes from her carefully constructed persona— the activist with a soft spot for silk saris, who travels the world, gives speeches, attends conferences, and mingles with policy-makers and celebrities. The one who says 'I am Laxmi' to the world. The one who's 'available and accessible, warm and friendly, strong and empowered'—this Laxmi 'doesn't give four fucks about anybody or anything, she talks to everybody, she is cool with everybody and everyone'. She is 'also me', Laxmi says, and adds, 'but she is for the world.' This persona 'opened doors for me, which had otherwise been firmly shut' and she offers certainty. This Laxmi is beyond gender—a true transgender who transcends gender, which is ultimately, quite simply 'a trap'.

But one that Laxmi understands only too well—in her most committed relationship with a man thus far, Laxmi understands how she's enslaved herself in the very trap she has detested all her life. How she rues patriarchy, and even though her very existence shakes its foundations, it's apparently the only way we know how to be as women. Even when we're channelling them. And yes, therein lies the rub, which is explored in the 'Love Monologue'. *Karyeshu dasi, karaneshu manthri; bhojeshu mata, shayaneshu rambha; roopeshu lakshmi, kshamayeshu dharitri; satkarma nari, kuladharma patni*—Laxmi quotes to me one evening, when she's talking about women and the multiple roles they play, while being true to each one. Such as the one of sister, which Prince Manvendra Singh Gohil, India's first openly gay member of royalty, spells out, with much love and fondness, in 'Laxmi, My Sister'.

'*Prakriti naari hai,*' she often likes to say. 'I think that's why I relate with femininity, because ultimately even men are part of prakriti and nothing can be bigger, or more all-encompassing.' This is the reason why this book is written primarily from a feminine perspective and the many *kirdaar*s of Laxmi's life, the men, and some women too, are viewed from the lens of the roles they have played in the shaping and forming of her mind and sensibility. And indeed how she views the world. The Creator is he who built her, and hence has knowledge and an awareness of her potential more so than herself. The Preserver is someone who Laxmi has grown with, someone who chiselled her, someone she drew her strength from. While the Destroyer is he who shakes the order—because to build anew and start again, you must first wreak complete and utter havoc.

As the cycle churns and lives are lived, there will always be new creators, preservers and destroyers. Laxmi will continue to encounter them, as she moves ahead and shines forth even brighter in the world, in the years to come. The fire in her belly and that searing ambition I was fortunate enough to witness up close—Laxmi is one person who means when she says, '*Taqdeer upar wala deta hai, apni tadbeer se apni taqdeer ko badalna padta hai.* You're destined to do things but you do need to create your own opportunities.'—will ensure that. Even when that means being in a constant tussle with the man inside her, explored in the form of 'Raju's Monologue' here, or striving against the demands of those around her, who create a veritable manthan for Laxmi, explored in 'The Churning of Laxmi'.

In the meantime, I hope this book with Laxmi at the centre of it urges and inspires us all to rethink our personal equations with who we are—our gender, our sexuality, and how we choose to define ourselves. And embrace the multiple identities that are possibilities. If not for ourselves, then for a better world, a greater legacy.

As a wise old meme told me, 'If you're out in public and you can't figure out a stranger's gender, follow these steps: 1. Don't worry about it.' I'd like to add: 2. Accept it. And 3. Open your mind, there's really nothing like it.

Besides, it's time.

* * *

Credit and gratitude where it's due—

If I have lived, for the better part of my formative years, in ignorance of there even being such a thing as a girl–boy divide, unaware that culture and society favoured one over the other, I only have my parents to thank. It is because of them that I think, feel, act the way I do, never once letting the fact of being a woman deter me in any way. And that despite having come across so many overbearing bearers of patriarchy, both men and women, in my adult life, I continue to never tone it down and 'adjust' just because it's assumed that, as a woman, I will.

For bestowing me with this power and moulding me so, thank you, Maa and Babba.

It was only fitting then that I chose to share my life and a lifetime of experiences with a man who's both yin and yang and hence, cool. The fact that we were drawn together in the first place was as serendipitous as it was fortuitous—truly meant to be. I'm grateful to be living my life with you, KJ.

Giving birth to a daughter formed and moulded me yet again. Harking back to my own childhood and shaping hers, I found myself grappling with norms, codes, expectations, stereotypes and then some, in the name of gender. I can safely say I would never have written this book if it weren't for her—the love of my life, my six-year-old Ahaana.

Encountering Laxmi has been a blessing for me—her spirit, joie de vivre, and courage have been an inspiration like no other. And quite simply, the book's raison d'être. Thank you, my dear author Laxmi, for trusting me to tell the world your story.

And to Premanka Goswami at Penguin—I'm deeply grateful that you thought of me when you envisioned this book. Thank you, also, for all the mazedaar gupshup around it. (And I still maintain that the dedication I texted you earlier was way better!)